Authentic Italian

recipes

written by Chef Mary Doe

Indulge in the authentic taste of Italy with "Authentic Italian Pasta Recipes: A Celebration of Timeless Flavors." Immerse yourself in the rich culinary heritage of Italy as you discover a collection of mouthwatering pasta recipes that have been cherished for generations. From classic favorites to regional specialties, this book is a tribute to the art of pasta-making and the vibrant flavors that define Italian cuisine. Get ready to elevate your cooking skills and transport your taste buds to the heart of Italy with these beloved pasta dishes.

Welcome to "Authentic Italian Pasta Recipes: A Culinary Journey Through Italy's Pasta Traditions." Get ready to indulge in the rich and diverse flavors of Italy as you explore the art of pasta-making and savor the authentic dishes that have captivated food lovers for generations.

In this meticulously curated collection, we invite you to discover the secrets of crafting perfect pasta dishes, from classic favorites to regional specialties. Immerse yourself in the aromas of fresh herbs, the velvety textures of homemade sauces, and the delightful combination of traditional ingredients that make Italian cuisine truly exceptional.

With step-by-step instructions, helpful tips, and vibrant photographs, this book serves as your personal guide to mastering the art of Italian pasta. From silky spaghetti carbonara to hearty lasagna Bolognese, each recipe is thoughtfully selected to showcase the timeless flavors and techniques that define Italian cooking.

Whether you're a seasoned home cook or a passionate food enthusiast, "Authentic Italian Pasta Recipes" invites you to embrace the essence of Italy's culinary heritage. So gather your loved ones, create lasting memories in the kitchen, and experience the joy of bringing these authentic Italian pasta dishes to life.

Get ready to embark on a delicious journey that will transport your taste buds straight to the heart of Italy. Buon appetito!

Chef Mary Doe

In this issue...

11 Linguine with Clam Sauce

13 Spaghetti Aglio e Olio

15 Penne alla Vodka

17 Lasagna

19 Spaghetti alla Carbonara

21 Fettuccine Alfredo

23 Spaghetti alla Puttanesca

25 Spaghetti with Meatballs

27 Shrimp Scampi Linguine

29 Gnocchi with Tomato Sauce

31 Pesto Pasta with Cherry Tomatoes and Mozzarella

33 Farfalle with Creamy Mushroom Sauce

35 Rigatoni with Sausage and Tomato Sauce

37 Pasta e Fagioli

39 Penne with Arrabbiata Sauce

Authentic

Linguine with Clam Sauce

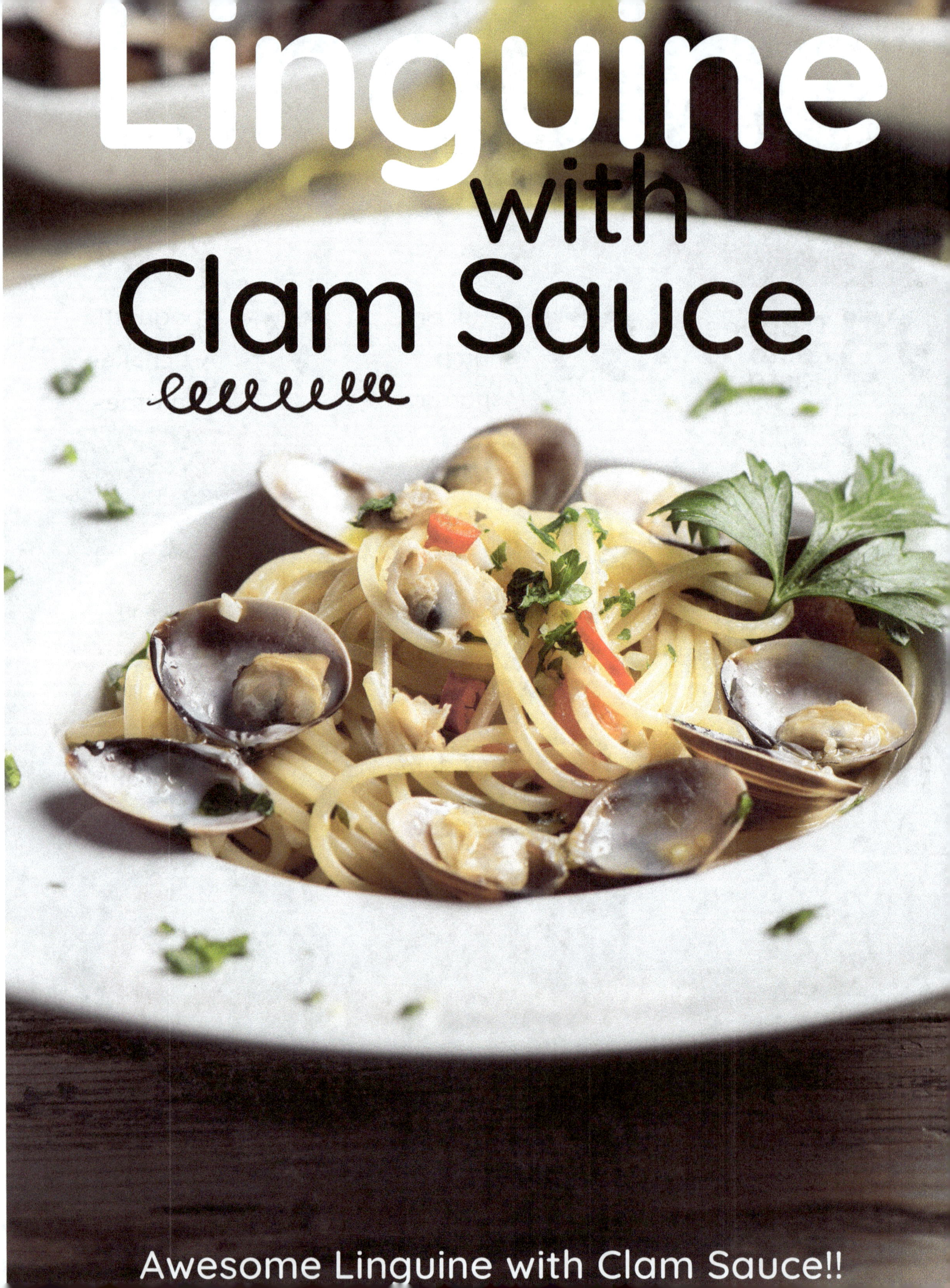

Awesome Linguine with Clam Sauce!!

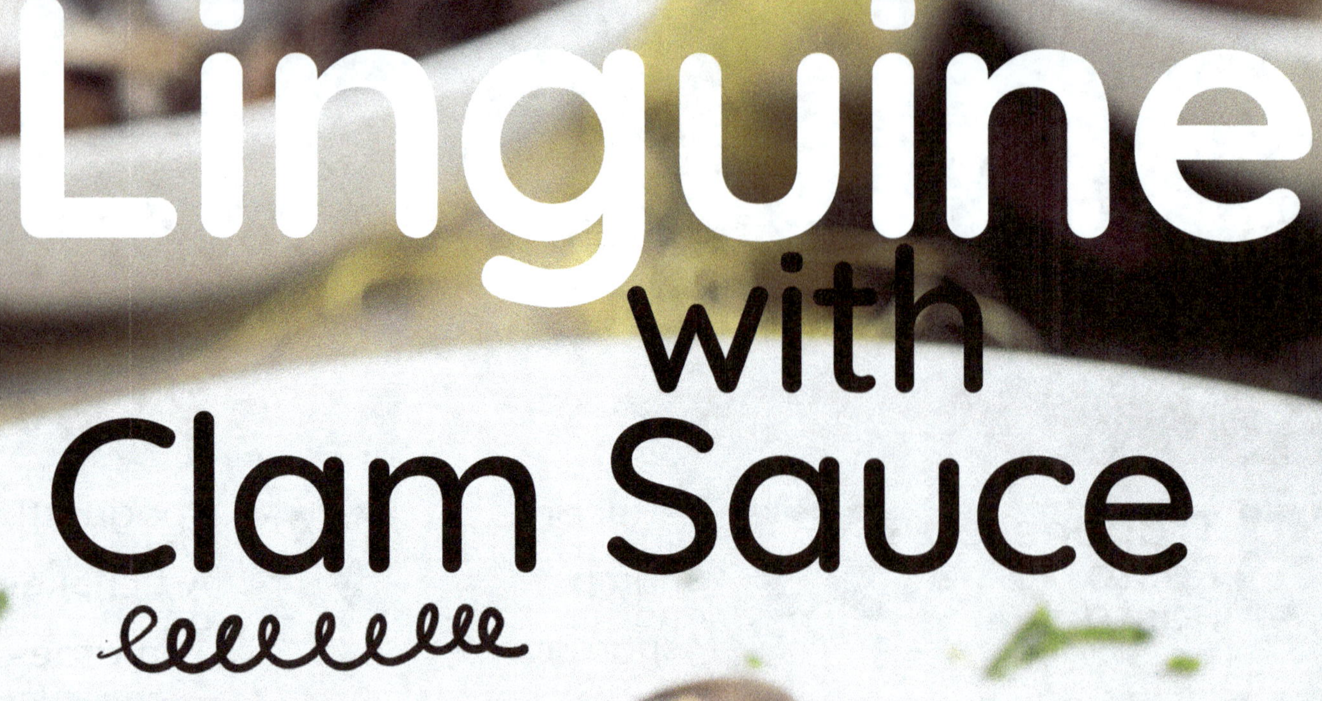

Linguine with Clam Sauce

Linguine with Clam Sauce is a classic Italian pasta dish that features a savory sauce made with fresh clams, garlic, white wine, and olive oil. The clams are cooked in the sauce until they open and release their briny juices, which infuse the sauce with incredible flavor. The linguine is cooked al dente and then tossed with the clam sauce, creating a delicious and comforting meal that is perfect for any occasion.

Cooking Information

4
Portions

35
Minutes

Easy
Difficulty

552
Calories

Ingredients

- 1 pound linguine pasta
- 2 pounds live clams, scrubbed and rinsed
- 4 cloves garlic, minced
- 1/2 teaspoon red pepper flakes
- 1/2 cup dry white wine
- 1/4 cup extra-virgin olive oil
- 1/4 cup chopped fresh parsley
- Salt and freshly ground black pepper, to taste

Execution

1. Bring a large pot of salted water to a boil. Add the linguine and cook according to package instructions until al dente, usually around 8-10 minutes. Reserve 1/2 cup of the pasta cooking water, then drain the pasta and set it aside.
2. In a large saucepan or pot, heat the olive oil over medium heat. Add the garlic and red pepper flakes and cook for 1-2 minutes, or until fragrant.
3. Add the clams and the white wine to the pan, then cover and cook for 5-7 minutes, or until the clams open. Discard any clams that don't open.
4. Remove the clams from the pan with a slotted spoon and set them aside. Add the reserved pasta cooking water to the pan and bring the sauce to a simmer.
5. Add the cooked linguine to the sauce and toss to coat evenly. Add the clams back into the pan and toss gently.
6. Divide the pasta and clams among four serving plates, then sprinkle with chopped parsley. Season with salt and pepper to taste.

Spaghetti Aglio e Olio

Spaghetti Aglio e Olio

X — X — x — X

Spaghetti Aglio e Olio is a simple yet delicious pasta dish that originated in Southern Italy. The name translates to "spaghetti with garlic and oil," which are the two main ingredients in the recipe. The spaghetti is cooked al dente and then tossed with a sauce made from olive oil, garlic, red pepper flakes, and parsley. The dish is usually served hot and garnished with additional parsley and grated Parmesan cheese. Despite its simplicity, Spaghetti Aglio e Olio is packed with bold and robust flavors that will satisfy any pasta lover.

Cooking Information

4
Portions

25
Minutes

Easy
Difficulty

506
Calories

Ingredients

- 1 pound spaghetti pasta
- 1/2 cup extra-virgin olive oil
- 6 cloves garlic, thinly sliced
- 1/2 teaspoon red pepper flakes
- 1/4 cup chopped fresh parsley
- Salt and freshly ground black pepper, to taste
- Grated Parmesan cheese, for serving (optional)

Execution

1. Bring a large pot of salted water to a boil. Add the spaghetti and cook according to package instructions until al dente, usually around 8-10 minutes. Reserve 1/2 cup of the pasta cooking water, then drain the pasta and set it aside.
2. While the pasta is cooking, heat the olive oil in a large skillet over medium heat. Add the garlic and red pepper flakes and cook for 1-2 minutes, or until the garlic is fragrant and lightly golden.
3. Remove the skillet from the heat and add the cooked spaghetti to the pan. Toss the spaghetti with the garlic oil until it is evenly coated.
4. If the pasta seems dry, add some of the reserved pasta cooking water to the skillet, a tablespoon at a time, until the desired consistency is achieved.
5. Add the chopped parsley to the spaghetti and toss to combine. Season with salt and black pepper to taste.
6. Divide the spaghetti among four serving plates, then top with grated Parmesan cheese (if using).

Awesome Penne alla Vodka !   Page 14

Penne alla Vodka

Penne alla Vodka is a popular Italian pasta dish that features penne pasta tossed in a creamy tomato-based sauce with a splash of vodka. The sauce is made by sautéing garlic and onions in butter, then adding canned tomatoes, heavy cream, and a generous pour of vodka. The penne pasta is cooked until al dente and then mixed with the sauce, resulting in a rich and flavorful pasta dish that is both savory and slightly sweet. Penne alla Vodka is a favorite of many Italian cuisine enthusiasts, and it's easy to see why - it's a delicious and indulgent meal that can be prepared in under 30 minutes.

Cooking Information

 6 Portions

 40 Minutes

 Easy Difficulty

 575 Calories

Ingredients

- 1 pound penne pasta
- 1 tablespoon olive oil
- 4 tablespoons unsalted butter
- 1 small onion, finely chopped
- 2 cloves garlic, minced
- 1/2 teaspoon red pepper flakes
- 1/2 cup vodka
- 1 (28-ounce) can crushed tomatoes
- 1 cup heavy cream
- Salt and freshly ground black pepper, to taste
- 1/4 cup chopped fresh parsley
- Grated Parmesan cheese, for serving (optional)

Execution

1. Bring a large pot of salted water to a boil. Add the penne pasta and cook according to package instructions until al dente, usually around 8-10 minutes. Reserve 1/2 cup of the pasta cooking water, then drain the pasta and set it aside.
2. While the pasta is cooking, heat the olive oil and butter in a large skillet over medium heat. Add the onion and garlic and cook until softened, about 5 minutes.
3. Add the red pepper flakes and vodka to the skillet and cook for 5 minutes, or until the vodka has reduced by half.
4. Add the crushed tomatoes to the skillet and bring the mixture to a simmer. Cook for 10-15 minutes, occasionally stirring until the sauce has thickened.
5. Add the heavy cream to the skillet and stir until it is fully incorporated into the sauce. Simmer for an additional 5 minutes, or until the sauce is heated through and slightly thickened.
6. Add the cooked penne pasta to the skillet with the sauce and toss until the pasta is evenly coated. If the pasta seems dry, add some of the reserved pasta cooking water to the skillet, a tablespoon at a time, until the desired consistency is achieved.
7. Season the pasta with salt and black pepper to taste, then sprinkle with chopped parsley. Serve hot, topped with grated Parmesan cheese if desired.

Lasagna

Lasagna

Lasagna is a classic Italian dish that is made up of layers of pasta sheets, meat sauce, and cheese. It is a comfort food that is loved by many, and it is perfect for feeding a crowd. The dish is assembled by layering cooked lasagna noodles with a rich tomato-based meat sauce and a creamy bechamel sauce, followed by a generous amount of mozzarella and Parmesan cheese. The layers are then baked until the cheese is melted and bubbly, resulting in a delicious and hearty meal that is perfect for any occasion. Lasagna can be made with different variations, including vegetable lasagna or using different meats, and it's a versatile dish that is sure to please any palate.

Cooking Information

10 Portions

1 Hour and 30 Minutes

Medium Difficulty

660 Calories

Ingredients

- 1 pound lasagna noodles
- 1 pound ground beef
- 1 onion, chopped
- 3 cloves garlic, minced
- 1 can (28 oz) crushed tomatoes
- 2 cans (6 oz each) tomato paste
- 2 tablespoons sugar
- 2 teaspoons salt
- 1 teaspoon dried basil leaves
- 1/2 teaspoon fennel seeds
- 1/4 teaspoon black pepper
- 4 cups shredded mozzarella cheese
- 1 1/2 cups grated Parmesan cheese
- 1 container (15 oz) ricotta cheese
- 2 eggs
- 1/4 cup chopped fresh parsley

Execution

1. Preheat the oven to 375°F.
2. Cook the lasagna noodles according to package instructions until al dente. Drain and set aside.
3. In a large skillet, brown the ground beef with the chopped onion and minced garlic until cooked through. Drain any excess fat.
4. Add the crushed tomatoes, tomato paste, sugar, salt, basil, fennel seeds, and black pepper to the skillet with the cooked beef. Simmer for 30 minutes, stirring occasionally.
5. In a separate bowl, mix together the ricotta cheese, eggs, and chopped parsley until well combined.
6. To assemble the lasagna, spread a layer of the meat sauce on the bottom of a 9x13 inch baking dish. Add a layer of cooked lasagna noodles on top of the sauce, followed by a layer of the ricotta cheese mixture and a layer of shredded mozzarella cheese. Repeat these layers until all ingredients are used up, ending with a layer of meat sauce on top.
7. Sprinkle the grated Parmesan cheese on top of the final layer of meat sauce.
8. Cover the baking dish with foil and bake for 25 minutes. Remove the foil and continue to bake for an additional 25 minutes, or until the cheese is melted and bubbly.
9. Let the lasagna cool for a few minutes before slicing and serving.

Spaghetti
alla Carbonara
Awesome Spaghetti alla Carbonara!!

Spaghetti alla Carbonara

Spaghetti alla carbonara is a popular Italian pasta dish that originated in Rome. It's made with spaghetti, eggs, pancetta or bacon, and cheese, and it has a creamy and velvety sauce that's both rich and savory. The sauce is made by whisking together eggs and cheese, and then mixing it with the hot pasta and crispy bacon or pancetta. The heat from the pasta cooks the eggs, creating a smooth and silky sauce that clings to the pasta. Spaghetti alla carbonara is a simple yet delicious meal that's perfect for any occasion, from a quick weeknight dinner to a fancy dinner party. It's a timeless classic that has been enjoyed for generations.

Cooking Information

4 Portions

15 Minutes

Easy Difficulty

660 Calories

Ingredients

- 1 lb spaghetti
- 6 oz pancetta or bacon, diced
- 4 large eggs
- 1 cup grated Parmesan cheese
- 2 garlic cloves, minced
- Salt and black pepper to taste
- 2 tbsp chopped parsley for garnish

Execution

1. Cook the spaghetti in a large pot of salted boiling water according to the package instructions. Reserve 1/2 cup of pasta water.
2. While the pasta is cooking, heat a large skillet over medium heat. Add the pancetta or bacon and cook until crispy, stirring occasionally.
3. In a mixing bowl, whisk together the eggs, grated Parmesan cheese, minced garlic, and a pinch of salt and black pepper.
4. Drain the cooked pasta and add it to the skillet with the crispy pancetta or bacon. Toss well to combine.
5. Remove the skillet from the heat and immediately add the egg and cheese mixture to the pasta. Stir quickly and continuously to coat the pasta with the egg and cheese mixture. Add reserved pasta water if needed to thin out the sauce.
6. Serve hot, garnished with chopped parsley.

Fettuccine
Alfredo
Awesome Fettuccine Alfredo!!

Fettuccine Alfredo

Fettuccine Alfredo is a classic Italian pasta dish that is known for its creamy and indulgent sauce. It's made with fettuccine pasta, butter, heavy cream, and Parmesan cheese, and sometimes garlic. The sauce is rich, smooth, and has a slight tanginess from the cheese. The pasta is typically cooked until it's al dente, and then tossed in the sauce until it's well coated. Fettuccine Alfredo is a comforting and satisfying meal that's perfect for a cozy night in or a special occasion. It's a decadent dish that has been enjoyed by pasta lovers around the world for many years.

Cooking Information

4
Portions

10
Minutes

Easy
Difficulty

940
Calories

Ingredients

- 1 lb fettuccine pasta
- 1 cup unsalted butter
- 2 cups heavy cream
- 2 cups grated Parmesan cheese
- 3 garlic cloves, minced
- Salt and black pepper to taste
- 2 tbsp chopped parsley for garnish

Execution

1. Cook the fettuccine pasta in a large pot of salted boiling water according to the package instructions.
2. While the pasta is cooking, melt the butter in a large saucepan over medium heat. Add the minced garlic and sauté for 1-2 minutes until fragrant.
3. Add the heavy cream to the saucepan and bring it to a simmer. Reduce the heat to low and stir in the grated Parmesan cheese until melted and smooth.
4. Drain the cooked pasta and add it to the saucepan with the Alfredo sauce. Toss well to combine.
5. Season with salt and black pepper to taste.
6. Serve hot, garnished with chopped parsley.

Spaghetti

alla Puttanesca

Spaghetti alla Puttanesca

Spaghetti alla Puttanesca is a classic Italian dish made with spaghetti pasta tossed in a flavorful sauce of tomatoes, olives, capers, garlic, and anchovies. The sauce has a slightly tangy and salty flavor that pairs perfectly with the spaghetti. This dish is quick and easy to make, and is perfect for a weeknight dinner or a casual get-together with friends and family.

Cooking Information

4 Portions

20 Minutes

Easy Difficulty

540 Calories

Ingredients

- 1 lb spaghetti pasta
- 1/4 cup extra-virgin olive oil
- 4 garlic cloves, minced
- 1/2 tsp red pepper flakes
- 1 can (28 oz) crushed tomatoes
- 1/2 cup pitted Kalamata olives, sliced
- 2 tbsp capers, rinsed and drained
- 4 anchovy fillets, minced
- Salt and black pepper to taste
- Fresh parsley, chopped, for garnish

Execution

1. Cook the spaghetti pasta in a large pot of salted boiling water according to the package instructions.
2. While the pasta is cooking, heat the olive oil in a large saucepan over medium heat. Add the minced garlic and red pepper flakes and sauté for 1-2 minutes until fragrant.
3. Add the crushed tomatoes to the saucepan and bring to a simmer. Add the sliced olives, capers, and anchovy fillets to the sauce and stir well to combine.
4. Let the sauce simmer for about 10-15 minutes, stirring occasionally, until it has thickened slightly.
5. Drain the cooked pasta and add it to the saucepan with the puttanesca sauce. Toss well to combine.
6. Season with salt and black pepper to taste.
7. Serve hot, garnished with chopped parsley.

Spaghetti
with Meatballs
Page 24

Spaghetti with Meatballs

Spaghetti with Meatballs is a classic Italian-American dish that features spaghetti pasta served with juicy, homemade meatballs and a rich tomato sauce. The meatballs are usually made with ground beef, breadcrumbs, and a variety of spices, and are simmered in the tomato sauce until tender and flavorful. This dish is hearty, comforting, and perfect for a family dinner or special occasion.

Cooking Information

4 Portions

1 hour 15 minutes

Easy Difficulty

780 Calories

Ingredients

- For the Meatballs:
- 1 lb ground beef
- 1/2 cup breadcrumbs
- 1/4 cup milk
- 1 egg, lightly beaten
- 2 cloves garlic, minced
- 1/4 cup grated Parmesan cheese
- 1 tbsp fresh parsley, chopped
- Salt and black pepper to taste
- Olive oil for frying
- For the Sauce:
- 1 can (28 oz) crushed tomatoes
- 2 cloves garlic, minced
- 1 tsp dried basil
- 1 tsp dried oregano
- Salt and black pepper to taste
- For the Spaghetti:
- 1 lb spaghetti pasta
- Salt for the pasta water
- Fresh parsley, chopped, for garnish
- Grated Parmesan cheese, for serving

Execution

1. In a large bowl, combine the ground beef, breadcrumbs, milk, beaten egg, minced garlic, grated Parmesan cheese, chopped parsley, and salt and pepper. Mix well with your hands until all ingredients are evenly incorporated.
2. Form the mixture into meatballs about 2 inches in diameter. Heat the olive oil in a large skillet over medium heat and add the meatballs. Cook until browned on all sides, about 8-10 minutes.
3. While the meatballs are cooking, make the sauce. In a large saucepan, combine the crushed tomatoes, minced garlic, dried basil, dried oregano, salt, and black pepper. Bring the mixture to a simmer and cook for 15-20 minutes until the sauce has thickened.
4. Add the cooked meatballs to the tomato sauce and continue to simmer for another 30-40 minutes until the meatballs are fully cooked and the sauce is rich and flavorful.
5. Cook the spaghetti pasta according to the package instructions in salted boiling water until al dente. Drain the pasta and toss it with the meatball sauce.
6. Serve hot, garnished with chopped parsley and grated Parmesan cheese.

Shrimp Scampi

Shrimp Scampi Linguine

Shrimp Scampi Linguine is a classic Italian-American dish that features succulent shrimp cooked in a garlic, butter, and white wine sauce served over a bed of linguine pasta. This dish is quick and easy to make, making it a great option for a weeknight dinner or a fancy dinner party.

Cooking Information

4 Portions

25 Minutes

Easy Difficulty

650 Calories

Ingredients

- 1 pound linguine pasta
- 1/2 cup unsalted butter
- 4 cloves garlic, minced
- 1/2 cup dry white wine
- 1/4 cup freshly squeezed lemon juice
- 1 pound large shrimp, peeled and deveined
- 1/4 cup chopped fresh parsley
- Salt and freshly ground black pepper, to taste
- 1/4 teaspoon red pepper flakes (optional)
- Grated Parmesan cheese, for serving

Execution

1. Cook the linguine pasta according to the package directions until al dente. Drain and set aside.
2. While the pasta is cooking, melt the butter in a large skillet over medium heat. Add the minced garlic and sauté for 1-2 minutes until fragrant.
3. Pour in the white wine and lemon juice, and stir to combine. Bring the mixture to a simmer and cook for 3-4 minutes until the liquid has reduced by half.
4. Add the shrimp to the skillet, and cook for 2-3 minutes until pink and cooked through.
5. Stir in the chopped parsley, salt, black pepper, and red pepper flakes (if using).
6. Add the cooked linguine to the skillet with the shrimp scampi sauce, and toss to combine.
7. Serve the Shrimp Scampi Linguine hot, garnished with grated Parmesan cheese.

Gnocchi
with Tomato Sauce

Gnocchi
with Tomato Sauce

Gnocchi with tomato sauce is a delicious and satisfying Italian dish that is easy to prepare and sure to please. Gnocchi are small, soft potato dumplings that are boiled until tender and then coated in a flavorful tomato sauce made with crushed tomatoes, garlic, onion, and herbs. The dish can be enjoyed on its own or served as a side dish to accompany your favorite meat or vegetable dishes. Gnocchi with tomato sauce is a versatile and comforting meal that is perfect for any season and sure to become a family favorite.

Cooking Information

4
Portions

20
Minutes

Medium
Difficulty

350
Calories

Ingredients

- 1 pound gnocchi
- 2 tablespoons olive oil
- 2 cloves garlic, minced
- 1/2 onion, diced
- 1 can (28 oz) crushed tomatoes
- 1/2 teaspoon dried basil
- 1/2 teaspoon dried oregano
- Salt and pepper, to taste
- Grated Parmesan cheese, for serving

Execution

1. Bring a large pot of salted water to a boil. Add the gnocchi and cook according to package instructions.
2. While the gnocchi is cooking, heat the olive oil in a large skillet over medium heat. Add the garlic and onion and sauté until softened, about 3-4 minutes.
3. Add the crushed tomatoes, basil, oregano, salt, and pepper. Bring to a simmer and cook for 10-15 minutes, until the sauce has thickened slightly.
4. Drain the gnocchi and add it to the skillet with the tomato sauce. Toss to coat the gnocchi in the sauce.
5. Serve the gnocchi with grated Parmesan cheese on top. Enjoy!

Pesto Pasta
with Cherry Tomatoes
and Mozzarella

Pesto Pasta with Cherry Tomatoes and Mozzarella

Pesto Pasta with Cherry Tomatoes and Mozzarella is a delightful and colorful dish that brings together the classic flavors of Italian cuisine. The fresh and tangy cherry tomatoes provide a burst of flavor that complements the smooth and creamy texture of the mozzarella cheese. The homemade pesto sauce adds a fragrant and herbaceous taste to the dish, while the pasta provides a satisfying base. This dish is not only visually appealing but also delicious, making it a perfect addition to any dinner table.

Cooking Information

4
Portions

12
Minutes

Easy
Difficulty

610
Calories

Ingredients

- 1 pound pasta (penne or fusilli)
- 2 cups cherry tomatoes, halved
- 1 cup fresh mozzarella cheese, cubed
- 2 cups fresh basil leaves
- 1/2 cup grated parmesan cheese
- 1/2 cup pine nuts
- 3 garlic cloves, minced
- 1/2 cup extra-virgin olive oil
- Salt and pepper to taste

Execution

1. Cook the pasta according to the package instructions until al dente.
2. While the pasta is cooking, prepare the pesto sauce. In a food processor or blender, combine the basil, parmesan cheese, pine nuts, garlic, and olive oil. Blend until smooth.
3. Drain the pasta and return it to the pot. Add the pesto sauce and stir until the pasta is coated evenly.
4. Add the cherry tomatoes and cubed mozzarella cheese to the pot and stir gently.
5. Season with salt and pepper to taste.
6. Serve hot and enjoy!

Farfalle
with Creamy
Mushroom Sauce

Farfalle with Creamy Mushroom Sauce

Farfalle with Creamy Mushroom Sauce is a comforting and flavorful pasta dish that combines the earthiness of mushrooms with a rich and creamy sauce. The farfalle pasta, also known as bowtie pasta, is the perfect shape to hold onto the delicious sauce and tender mushrooms. It's a simple yet impressive dish that's perfect for a cozy dinner at home.

Cooking Information

4 Portions

30 Minutes

Easy Difficulty

600 Calories

Ingredients

- 1 lb farfalle pasta
- 2 tbsp olive oil
- 1 lb mushrooms, sliced
- 4 cloves garlic, minced
- 1 cup heavy cream
- 1/2 cup grated Parmesan cheese
- Salt and pepper to taste
- Fresh parsley for garnish

Execution

1. Cook the farfalle pasta according to package directions until al dente. Drain and set aside.
2. In a large pan, heat the olive oil over medium-high heat. Add the sliced mushrooms and sauté for 5-7 minutes until they are golden brown.
3. Add the minced garlic to the pan and sauté for an additional minute.
4. Pour in the heavy cream and stir well. Add the grated Parmesan cheese and stir until it has melted and the sauce is smooth.
5. Reduce the heat to low and let the sauce simmer for 5-7 minutes, stirring occasionally, until it has thickened.
6. Season the sauce with salt and pepper to taste.
7. Add the cooked farfalle pasta to the sauce and toss until it is well coated.
8. Serve hot, garnished with fresh parsley.

Rigatoni
with Sausage and
Tomato Sauce
Page 34

Rigatoni with Sausage and Tomato Sauce

Rigatoni with Sausage and Tomato Sauce is a delicious and filling pasta dish that is perfect for any night of the week. This classic Italian recipe is made with rigatoni pasta and a flavorful tomato sauce that is cooked with spicy Italian sausage, garlic, and onions. The sausage infuses the sauce with a rich and savory flavor, while the rigatoni holds the sauce well, creating a deliciously satisfying meal. This dish is perfect for serving to guests or for a cozy family dinner.

Cooking Information

4-6 Portions

45 Minutes

Medium Difficulty

550 Calories

Ingredients

- 1 lb rigatoni pasta
- 1 lb Italian sausage, casing removed
- 1 can (28 oz) crushed tomatoes
- 1 onion, chopped
- 4 cloves garlic, minced
- 2 tbsp tomato paste
- 1/2 cup chicken broth
- 1 tsp dried oregano
- 1 tsp dried basil
- 1/4 tsp red pepper flakes
- Salt and pepper, to taste
- 2 tbsp olive oil
- Parmesan cheese, grated, for serving

Execution

1. Cook the rigatoni according to the package instructions until al dente. Drain and set aside.
2. Heat the olive oil in a large saucepan over medium heat. Add the sausage and cook, breaking it up with a wooden spoon, until browned and cooked through, about 8-10 minutes.
3. Add the chopped onion to the pan with the sausage and cook until softened, about 5 minutes. Add the minced garlic and cook for an additional minute.
4. Stir in the tomato paste, crushed tomatoes, chicken broth, dried oregano, dried basil, red pepper flakes, and salt and pepper to taste.
5. Bring the sauce to a simmer and let it cook for 10-15 minutes, stirring occasionally, until it has thickened.
6. Add the cooked rigatoni to the pan with the sauce and toss to coat. Serve hot with grated Parmesan cheese on top. Enjoy!

Pasta
e Fagioli
Awesome Pasta e Fagioli

Pasta e Fagioli

Pasta e Fagioli is a traditional Italian soup made with pasta and beans, and is a comfort food enjoyed by many. This hearty soup is packed with protein and fiber, making it a nutritious and filling meal. The pasta and beans are simmered in a tomato-based broth, along with savory herbs and spices, and can be customized to include vegetables and meats. It's a perfect dish for cooler weather or when you're in the mood for a comforting bowl of soup.

Cooking Information

4-6 Portions

30 Minutes

Easy Difficulty

275 Calories

Ingredients

- 1 can (15 oz) cannellini beans, drained and rinsed
- 1 can (14.5 oz) diced tomatoes, undrained
- 4 cups chicken or vegetable broth
- 2 tablespoons olive oil
- 1 onion, chopped
- 3 cloves garlic, minced
- 2 carrots, peeled and diced
- 2 stalks celery, diced
- 1 teaspoon dried oregano
- 1/2 teaspoon dried basil
- Salt and pepper, to taste
- 1 cup small pasta (such as ditalini, elbow macaroni, or small shells)
- Grated Parmesan cheese, for serving

Execution

1. In a large pot, heat the olive oil over medium heat. Add the onion, garlic, carrots, and celery, and cook until softened, about 5 minutes.
2. Add the diced tomatoes, broth, oregano, basil, salt, and pepper. Bring to a boil, then reduce heat and let simmer for 10 minutes.
3. Add the cannellini beans and pasta to the pot. Cook for an additional 10-12 minutes, or until the pasta is cooked to your liking.
4. Serve hot, topped with grated Parmesan cheese.

Penne with
Arrabbiata Sauce
Page 38

Penne with Arrabbiata Sauce

Penne with Arrabbiata Sauce is a spicy and flavorful pasta dish that originated in Italy. The sauce is made with tomatoes, garlic, red chili flakes, and olive oil, giving it a fiery kick that is balanced by the sweetness of the tomatoes. The penne pasta is tossed with the Arrabbiata sauce and topped with fresh herbs and grated Parmesan cheese, making it a simple yet delicious meal that can be made in a short amount of time.

Cooking Information

4 Portions

30 minutes

Easy Difficulty

425 Calories

Ingredients

- 1 lb penne pasta
- 2 tbsp olive oil
- 4 garlic cloves, minced
- 1/2 tsp red pepper flakes
- 28 oz canned diced tomatoes
- 1/4 cup fresh basil, chopped
- salt and pepper to taste
- 1/4 cup grated Parmesan cheese (optional)

Execution

1. Cook penne according to package instructions in a large pot of salted boiling water until al dente. Reserve 1 cup of the pasta water, then drain the pasta.
2. In a large skillet, heat olive oil over medium heat. Add minced garlic and red pepper flakes, cook until fragrant for about 1 minute.
3. Add canned diced tomatoes to the skillet with the garlic and red pepper flakes. Let it simmer for about 10-15 minutes or until the sauce has thickened slightly.
4. Add salt and pepper to taste.
5. Once the sauce is ready, add the cooked penne pasta to the skillet and toss it with the sauce. If the sauce is too thick, use the reserved pasta water to thin it out.
6. Finally, sprinkle chopped basil on top and grated Parmesan cheese (optional) and serve hot. Enjoy!

Orecchiette
with Broccoli and
Anchovy Sauce

Orecchiette with Broccoli and Anchovy Sauce

Orecchiette with Broccoli and Anchovy Sauce is a savory and satisfying pasta dish that brings together the flavors of tender broccoli florets and salty anchovy sauce. The pasta is cooked until al dente and then tossed with the sauce made with olive oil, garlic, and anchovy fillets. The broccoli florets are then added to the sauce, allowing them to cook until they are tender and infused with the delicious flavors of the sauce. The dish is finished with a sprinkle of Parmesan cheese for added depth of flavor.

Cooking Information

 4 Portions

 25 minutes

 Easy Difficulty

 550 Calories

Ingredients

- 1 lb orecchiette pasta
- 2 heads broccoli, cut into small florets
- 1/2 cup olive oil
- 6 garlic cloves, minced
- 6 anchovy fillets, chopped
- 1/2 tsp red pepper flakes
- Salt and black pepper to taste
- Grated Parmesan cheese for serving

Execution

1. Cook the orecchiette pasta in a large pot of salted boiling water, according to package instructions. Reserve 1/2 cup of the pasta water before draining.
2. While the pasta is cooking, heat the olive oil in a large skillet over medium heat. Add the garlic, anchovies, and red pepper flakes, and cook for 2-3 minutes until fragrant.
3. Add the broccoli florets to the skillet and stir to combine. Cook for 5-7 minutes until the broccoli is tender.
4. Add the cooked pasta to the skillet with the broccoli and anchovy sauce. Toss to combine, adding reserved pasta water as needed to thin out the sauce.
5. Season with salt and black pepper to taste.
6. Serve hot, topped with grated Parmesan cheese.

Bucatini
with Pancetta and Peas

Bucatini with Pancetta and Peas

Bucatini with Pancetta and Peas is a classic Italian pasta dish that combines the salty flavor of pancetta with the sweet taste of peas in a creamy sauce. This easy-to-make recipe is perfect for a quick weeknight dinner or a cozy meal with friends and family. The bucatini, a thick spaghetti-like pasta, provides the perfect texture to hold up to the rich sauce, while the peas add a pop of freshness and color to the dish. With its simple ingredients and bold flavors, this pasta dish is sure to become a favorite in your recipe collection.

Cooking Information

4 Portions

25 minutes

Easy Difficulty

550 Calories

Ingredients

- 1 lb. bucatini pasta
- 1 cup frozen peas
- 4 oz. pancetta, diced
- 1 small onion, chopped
- 2 cloves garlic, minced
- 1/2 cup chicken broth
- 1/2 cup heavy cream
- 1/2 cup grated Parmesan cheese
- Salt and pepper to taste

Execution

1. Cook the bucatini pasta according to package instructions until al dente. Reserve 1 cup of pasta water.
2. In a large skillet over medium-high heat, cook the pancetta until crisp. Remove the pancetta from the skillet and set aside.
3. In the same skillet, sauté the onion and garlic until softened.
4. Add the frozen peas and chicken broth to the skillet. Bring to a boil and cook for 2-3 minutes.
5. Reduce heat to low and add the heavy cream to the skillet. Simmer for 5-6 minutes or until the sauce has thickened.
6. Add the cooked bucatini pasta, reserved pasta water, and grated Parmesan cheese to the skillet. Toss until well combined.
7. Stir in the cooked pancetta and season with salt and pepper to taste.
8. Serve hot and enjoy!

Zucchini carbonara

Zucchini Carbonara

Zucchini Carbonara is a delicious and healthier twist on the classic Carbonara pasta dish. Instead of using bacon or pancetta, this recipe uses zucchini to add a fresh and nutritious element to the dish. The creamy egg-based sauce, combined with the savory flavor of grated Parmesan cheese and the slight sweetness of sautéed zucchini, creates a perfect balance of flavors that will leave you wanting more. This recipe is perfect for anyone looking for a healthier and lighter version of the traditional Carbonara pasta dish.

Cooking Information

4 Portions

30 minutes

Easy Difficulty

500 Calories

Ingredients

- 12 oz. spaghetti
- 4 slices of bacon, diced
- 1 large zucchini, grated
- 1/2 cup grated Parmesan cheese
- 3 egg yolks
- 1/2 cup heavy cream
- Salt and pepper to taste
- Fresh parsley for garnish

Execution

1. Cook the spaghetti according to the package instructions until al dente.
2. In a large pan, cook the bacon over medium heat until crispy. Remove the bacon from the pan and set aside, leaving the bacon grease in the pan.
3. Add the grated zucchini to the pan with the bacon grease and cook for 5-7 minutes until the zucchini is softened.
4. In a mixing bowl, whisk together the egg yolks, heavy cream, and Parmesan cheese until well combined.
5. Drain the spaghetti and add it to the pan with the zucchini. Toss the spaghetti and zucchini together to combine.
6. Turn off the heat and pour the egg and cream mixture over the spaghetti and zucchini, tossing everything together quickly to combine.
7. Add the crispy bacon back to the pan and toss everything together.
8. Serve hot, garnished with fresh parsley and a sprinkle of additional Parmesan cheese, if desired. Enjoy!

Spicy Sausage
and Peppers Rigatoni

Spicy Sausage and Peppers Rigatoni

Spicy Sausage and Peppers Rigatoni is a classic Italian pasta dish that's perfect for a hearty and flavorful meal. The dish features rigatoni pasta tossed with spicy Italian sausage, sweet bell peppers, and tangy tomato sauce. The combination of these bold flavors creates a deliciously satisfying and comforting meal that's perfect for any occasion.

Cooking Information

 4-6 Portions

 30 Minutes

 Easy Difficulty

 600 Calories

Ingredients

- 1 pound rigatoni pasta
- 1 pound spicy Italian sausage, casings removed
- 1 red bell pepper, sliced
- 1 green bell pepper, sliced
- 1 medium onion, diced
- 4 cloves garlic, minced
- 1 can (28 ounces) crushed tomatoes
- 1/2 cup chicken broth
- 2 teaspoons dried basil
- 1 teaspoon dried oregano
- 1/2 teaspoon red pepper flakes
- Salt and pepper to taste
- Parmesan cheese for topping

Execution

1. Cook rigatoni pasta according to package directions until al dente.
2. In a large skillet over medium-high heat, cook sausage until browned and cooked through. Use a slotted spoon to remove the sausage from the skillet and set aside.
3. In the same skillet, add the bell peppers, onion, and garlic. Cook until the vegetables are tender, stirring occasionally.
4. Add the crushed tomatoes, chicken broth, dried basil, dried oregano, red pepper flakes, and cooked sausage to the skillet. Stir to combine and let the sauce simmer for 10-15 minutes until slightly thickened.
5. Drain the rigatoni pasta and add it to the skillet with the sauce. Toss to coat the pasta with the sauce.
6. Serve hot, topped with grated Parmesan cheese.

Chicken
Alfredo
Page 48

Chicken Alfredo

Chicken Alfredo is a classic pasta dish that combines tender pieces of chicken with a rich and creamy Alfredo sauce. The dish is usually made with fettuccine pasta, but it can be made with other pasta shapes as well. The chicken is seasoned with Italian herbs and spices, then seared until golden brown and cooked through. The Alfredo sauce is made with heavy cream, butter, garlic, and Parmesan cheese, and is seasoned with salt and pepper to taste. The sauce is then tossed with the cooked pasta and chicken, and garnished with fresh parsley and additional grated Parmesan cheese. Chicken Alfredo is a comforting and satisfying dish that is perfect for a cozy night in or a special occasion

Cooking Information

4
Portions

20
Minutes

Easy
Difficulty

795
Calories

Ingredients

- 1 lb fettuccine pasta
- 2 boneless, skinless chicken breasts, sliced
- 2 cloves garlic, minced
- 1 cup heavy cream
- 1/2 cup grated Parmesan cheese
- Salt and pepper, to taste
- 2 tbsp olive oil
- Fresh parsley, chopped, for garnish

Execution

1. Cook fettuccine pasta according to package instructions until al dente. Reserve 1/2 cup of pasta water before draining.
2. In a separate pan, heat olive oil over medium-high heat. Add chicken and cook until browned and cooked through, about 5-7 minutes.
3. Add minced garlic to the pan with the chicken and cook for 1-2 minutes, until fragrant.
4. Reduce heat to low and pour in heavy cream. Stir to combine with chicken and garlic.
5. Add grated Parmesan cheese to the pan and stir until cheese is melted and sauce is smooth.
6. Season sauce with salt and pepper to taste.
7. Add cooked fettuccine to the pan with the sauce, along with the reserved pasta water. Toss to coat pasta with the sauce.
8. Serve chicken Alfredo hot, garnished with chopped fresh parsley.

Awesome Rigatoni!!

Rigatoni with Eggplant and Ricotta

✗ — ✗ — ✗ — ✗

This hearty pasta dish is perfect for a cozy weeknight dinner. Rigatoni pasta is tossed with tender chunks of roasted eggplant, tangy tomato sauce, and creamy ricotta cheese. The combination of textures and flavors in this dish is sure to please any pasta lover. It's a great way to incorporate more vegetables into your diet without sacrificing taste.

Cooking Information

4-6
Portions

45
Minutes

Easy
Difficulty

440
Calories

Ingredients

- 1 pound rigatoni pasta
- 1 large eggplant, diced
- 1 cup ricotta cheese
- 2 cloves garlic, minced
- 1 can crushed tomatoes
- 1/4 cup fresh basil leaves, chopped
- 1/4 cup grated Parmesan cheese
- 2 tablespoons olive oil
- Salt and pepper to taste

Execution

1. Cook the rigatoni according to the package directions until al dente. Drain and set aside.
2. In a large pan, heat the olive oil over medium heat. Add the diced eggplant and cook for about 8-10 minutes or until softened.
3. Add the minced garlic to the pan and cook for another minute.
4. Pour the can of crushed tomatoes into the pan, along with the chopped basil leaves, and season with salt and pepper to taste. Simmer for about 10-12 minutes or until the sauce has thickened.
5. Stir in the cooked rigatoni and mix well with the sauce.
6. In a separate bowl, mix together the ricotta cheese and grated Parmesan cheese.
7. Serve the rigatoni topped with dollops of the ricotta mixture.
8. Enjoy your delicious and easy-to-make Rigatoni with Eggplant and Ricotta!

Spaghetti

Bolognese

Page 52

Spaghetti Bolognese

Spaghetti Bolognese is a classic Italian dish that has become popular all around the world. It consists of spaghetti noodles served with a hearty meat sauce made with ground beef, tomato sauce, and seasonings. The sauce is simmered for hours, allowing the flavors to meld together and create a rich, savory taste that is both satisfying and comforting. Spaghetti Bolognese is a timeless dish that is perfect for a family dinner or a casual gathering with friends.

Cooking Information

4-6 Portions

45 minutes

Medium Difficulty

540 Calories

Ingredients

- 500g spaghetti
- 500g ground beef
- 1 onion, chopped
- 2 cloves garlic, minced
- 2 carrots, diced
- 2 celery stalks, diced
- 1 can (400g) crushed tomatoes
- 2 tbsp tomato paste
- 1 cup beef broth
- 2 tbsp olive oil
- 1 tsp dried basil
- 1 tsp dried oregano
- Salt and black pepper, to taste
- Grated parmesan cheese, for serving

Execution

1. Cook spaghetti according to package instructions until al dente. Drain and set aside.
2. In a large pot or Dutch oven, heat olive oil over medium-high heat. Add onion, garlic, carrots, and celery, and cook until softened, about 5 minutes.
3. Add ground beef and cook, breaking up with a wooden spoon, until browned and no longer pink.
4. Stir in crushed tomatoes, tomato paste, beef broth, basil, oregano, salt, and pepper. Bring to a simmer and let cook for 20-25 minutes, stirring occasionally.
5. Serve spaghetti topped with bolognese sauce and grated parmesan cheese.

Farfalle
with Smoked Salmon
and Cream Sauce

Farfalle with Smoked Salmon and Cream Sauce

Farfalle with Smoked Salmon and Cream Sauce is a delicious and sophisticated pasta dish that is perfect for a special occasion or romantic dinner. The creamy sauce, made with heavy cream, Parmesan cheese, and white wine, perfectly complements the smoky flavor of the salmon. The bowtie-shaped pasta, or farfalle, is a great choice for this dish as it catches and holds onto the sauce and chunks of salmon. This dish is sure to impress any pasta and seafood lover.

Cooking Information

4-6 Portions

20 Minutes

Easy Difficulty

600 Calories

Ingredients

- 1 pound farfalle pasta
- 1/2 cup unsalted butter
- 1 cup heavy cream
- 1/2 cup grated Parmesan cheese
- 1/2 cup smoked salmon, chopped
- 1/4 cup fresh parsley, chopped
- Salt and pepper, to taste

Execution

1. Cook the farfalle pasta according to the package directions until al dente. Drain and set aside.
2. In a large saucepan, melt the butter over medium heat. Add the heavy cream and Parmesan cheese, stirring constantly until the cheese is melted and the mixture is smooth.
3. Add the chopped smoked salmon to the saucepan and stir to combine. Cook for 2-3 minutes until the salmon is heated through.
4. Add the cooked farfalle pasta to the saucepan and toss to coat with the sauce. Cook for an additional 1-2 minutes until the pasta is heated through.
5. Season with salt and pepper to taste. Serve the pasta hot, garnished with chopped parsley.

Fettuccine
with Mushroom Sauce

Fettuccine with Mushroom Sauce

Fettuccine with Mushroom Sauce is a classic Italian pasta dish that is simple yet delicious. The rich and creamy mushroom sauce perfectly coats the al dente fettuccine, creating a comforting and satisfying meal. This dish is perfect for a cozy dinner at home or a special occasion, and is sure to please both mushroom lovers and pasta enthusiasts alike.

Cooking Information

4 Portions

30 Minutes

Easy Difficulty

642 Calories

Ingredients

- 1 lb fettuccine pasta
- 2 tbsp butter
- 1 tbsp olive oil
- 1 lb fresh mushrooms, sliced
- 3 cloves garlic, minced
- 1 cup heavy cream
- 1/2 cup grated Parmesan cheese
- Salt and pepper to taste
- Fresh parsley for garnish

Execution

1. Bring a large pot of salted water to a boil. Add the fettuccine pasta and cook according to package directions until al dente. Drain the pasta and set it aside.
2. While the pasta cooks, melt the butter and olive oil in a large pan over medium heat. Add the sliced mushrooms and sauté for 5-7 minutes until they are soft and golden brown. Add the minced garlic and cook for an additional minute.
3. Pour the heavy cream into the pan and stir until the sauce is heated through. Add the grated Parmesan cheese and stir until it is melted and fully incorporated into the sauce. Season with salt and pepper to taste.
4. Add the cooked fettuccine to the mushroom sauce and toss until the pasta is coated in the sauce. Cook for an additional minute or two until the pasta is heated through.
5. Serve the fettuccine with mushroom sauce hot, garnished with fresh parsley. Enjoy!

Linguine
alle Vongole

Linguine alle Vongole

Linguine alle Vongole is a classic Italian dish consisting of linguine pasta cooked with fresh clams in a garlic and white wine sauce. The dish is typically prepared with either baby clams or larger, meatier clams such as Manila or Littleneck clams. The pasta is cooked al dente and tossed with the clams, garlic, white wine, and a touch of red pepper flakes for a subtle kick of heat. This seafood pasta dish is a perfect blend of simple, yet delicious flavors and is a favorite among seafood lovers.

Cooking Information

4 Portions

20 Minutes

Medium Dificulty

600 Calories

Ingredients

- 1 pound linguine pasta
- 2 pounds fresh clams, cleaned
- 4 cloves garlic, minced
- 1/2 teaspoon red pepper flakes
- 1/2 cup white wine
- 1/4 cup olive oil
- 1/4 cup chopped fresh parsley
- Salt and pepper, to taste

Execution

1. Bring a large pot of salted water to a boil. Add the linguine and cook according to the package instructions until al dente.
2. While the pasta is cooking, heat the olive oil in a large skillet over medium heat. Add the garlic and red pepper flakes, and cook until the garlic is fragrant, about 1 minute.
3. Add the clams and white wine to the skillet, and cover. Cook until the clams have opened, about 5-7 minutes.
4. Drain the pasta and add it to the skillet with the clams and their juices. Toss to combine.
5. Add the chopped parsley, and season with salt and pepper to taste. Serve hot.

Farfalle
al Limone

Farfalle al Limone

Farfalle al Limone is a refreshing and vibrant pasta dish that combines the delicate flavors of lemon, garlic, and Parmesan cheese. This elegant recipe brings a burst of citrusy goodness to your plate, elevating your dining experience with its light and zesty profile.

The tender farfalle pasta, also known as bow-tie pasta, perfectly captures the velvety lemon-infused sauce, creating a harmonious blend of flavors in every bite. The addition of garlic adds a subtle kick, while the grated Parmesan cheese provides a creamy richness that beautifully balances the tangy lemon.

Whether enjoyed as a main course or served as a side dish, Farfalle al Limone is a versatile and easy-to-make pasta dish that impresses with its simplicity and bright flavors. It's a delightful option for a quick weeknight meal or a special occasion, leaving a lasting impression on your palate and leaving you craving more.

Indulge in the vibrant essence of this classic Italian pasta dish and let the tantalizing combination of lemon and Parmesan transport you to the sunny Mediterranean coast. With its refreshing taste and charming presentation, Farfalle al Limone is sure to become a favorite in your pasta repertoire.

Cooking Information

4 Portions

25 Minutes

Easy Dificulty

450 Calories

Ingredients

- 12 ounces farfalle pasta
- 2 tablespoons unsalted butter
- 2 cloves garlic, minced
- Zest of 1 lemon
- Juice of 1 lemon
- 1 cup heavy cream
- 1/2 cup grated Parmesan cheese
- Salt and pepper to taste
- Fresh parsley, chopped (for garnish)

Execution

1. Cook the farfalle pasta according to the package instructions until al dente. Drain and set aside.
2. In a large skillet, melt the butter over medium heat. Add the minced garlic and sauté for 1-2 minutes until fragrant.
3. Add the lemon zest and lemon juice to the skillet, stirring well to combine with the garlic and butter.
4. Pour in the heavy cream and bring the mixture to a simmer. Cook for 2-3 minutes, stirring occasionally, until the sauce slightly thickens.
5. Stir in the grated Parmesan cheese until melted and well incorporated into the sauce. Season with salt and pepper to taste.
6. Add the cooked farfalle pasta to the skillet, tossing gently to coat the pasta evenly with the lemon cream sauce.
7. Remove from heat and serve the Farfalle al Limone in individual bowls or plates. Garnish with freshly chopped parsley for an extra burst of freshness.
8. Enjoy this delightful pasta dish immediately, while it's still hot and creamy.
9. Note: You can customize this recipe by adding grilled chicken, shrimp, or your favorite vegetables for added protein and texture.

Rigatoni
alla Genovese

Rigatoni alla Genovese

Rigatoni alla Genovese is a classic Italian pasta dish hailing from the city of Genoa in northern Italy. The dish features rigatoni pasta tossed in a hearty and flavorful meat sauce made with tender beef, sweet onions, and aromatic herbs. The beef is slow-cooked until it is melt-in-your-mouth tender, and the onions are caramelized to release their natural sweetness. The pasta is then tossed with the meat sauce and topped with a generous helping of grated Parmesan cheese. The result is a delicious and comforting pasta dish that is perfect for any occasion.

Cooking Information

4-6 Portions

3-4 Hours

Moderate Dificulty

650 Calories

Ingredients

- 1 lb rigatoni pasta
- 2 lbs beef chuck roast, cut into small cubes
- 1 lb yellow onions, chopped
- 2 cloves garlic, minced
- 1 cup beef broth
- 1 cup white wine
- 1 cup grated Parmesan cheese
- 2 tbsp tomato paste
- 3 tbsp extra-virgin olive oil
- Salt and pepper to taste

Execution

1. Heat the olive oil in a large pot over medium-high heat. Add the onions and garlic and sauté until soft and fragrant, about 5 minutes.
2. Add the beef to the pot and season with salt and pepper. Brown the beef on all sides, about 10 minutes.
3. Add the tomato paste and cook for another 2-3 minutes.
4. Add the beef broth and white wine to the pot and bring to a boil. Reduce heat to low and simmer for 2-3 hours, or until the beef is tender and the sauce has thickened.
5. Cook the rigatoni pasta according to package instructions until al dente. Drain the pasta and reserve about 1 cup of the pasta water.
6. Add the cooked pasta and reserved pasta water to the pot with the beef and sauce. Toss until the pasta is coated in the sauce.
7. Stir in the grated Parmesan cheese and serve hot.

Bucatini
with Garlic and Oil

Bucatini with Garlic and Oil

Bucatini with Garlic and Olive Oil is a classic Italian pasta dish that is simple, yet bursting with flavor. This dish features al dente bucatini pasta tossed in a fragrant garlic-infused olive oil, creating a rich and aromatic sauce that coats the pasta strands. The dish is finished with a sprinkle of red pepper flakes for a hint of spice, adding an extra kick to the dish. Bucatini with Garlic and Olive Oil is a perfect example of how a few quality ingredients can come together to create a delicious and satisfying pasta dish. Whether you're a garlic lover or simply appreciate the beauty of a well-executed pasta dish, this recipe is sure to become a favorite in your culinary repertoire.

Cooking Information

2
Portions

12
minutes

Easy
Difficulty

400
Calories

Ingredients

- 8 oz bucatini pasta
- 4 cloves garlic, thinly sliced
- 1/4 cup extra-virgin olive oil
- 1/2 tsp red pepper flakes (adjust to taste)
- Salt and black pepper to taste
- Fresh parsley, chopped (optional)
- Grated Pecorino Romano or Parmesan cheese for serving (optional)

Execution

1. Bring a large pot of salted water to a boil. Cook the bucatini pasta according to package instructions until al dente. Drain and set aside.
2. In a large skillet, heat the olive oil over medium heat. Add the thinly sliced garlic and red pepper flakes, and sauté for 2-3 minutes until the garlic is fragrant and lightly golden. Be careful not to burn the garlic.
3. Add the cooked bucatini pasta to the skillet with the garlic oil. Toss the pasta in the oil to coat evenly. Season with salt and black pepper to taste.
4. Cook the pasta in the skillet for another 2-3 minutes, stirring occasionally, until heated through and lightly crispy on the edges.
5. Remove from heat and transfer the Bucatini with Garlic and Olive Oil to serving plates. Garnish with chopped fresh parsley, if desired.
6. Serve hot, optionally topped with grated Pecorino Romano or Parmesan cheese for added flavor.

Penne
with Zucchini
and Tomato Sauce

Penne with Zucchini and Tomato Sauce

Penne with Zucchini and Tomato Sauce is a classic Italian pasta dish that's perfect for those who love the combination of fresh vegetables and tangy tomato flavors. Cooked penne pasta is tossed with sautéed zucchini, garlic, and a simple tomato sauce, creating a light and flavorful meal that's both satisfying and nutritious. With its quick and easy preparation, this dish is a fantastic option for busy weeknight dinners or as a side dish for a larger meal. Enjoy the taste of Italy in every bite with this delicious penne pasta recipe! Buon appetito!

Cooking Information

4
Portions

25
minutes

Easy
Difficulty

350
Calories

Ingredients

- 8 oz penne pasta
- 2 medium zucchini, sliced
- 2 cloves garlic, minced
- 1 can (14 oz) diced tomatoes
- 1 tbsp olive oil
- 1/2 tsp red pepper flakes (optional)
- Salt and pepper to taste
- Freshly grated Parmesan cheese for serving (optional)
- Fresh basil leaves for garnish (optional)

Execution

1. Cook penne pasta according to package instructions until al dente. Drain and set aside.
2. In a large skillet, heat olive oil over medium heat. Add minced garlic and red pepper flakes (if using) and sauté for 1-2 minutes until fragrant.
3. Add sliced zucchini to the skillet and cook for 3-4 minutes until slightly softened.
4. Add diced tomatoes with their juice to the skillet, along with a pinch of salt and pepper. Stir to combine and bring to a simmer.
5. Reduce heat to low and let the sauce simmer for 10-15 minutes, stirring occasionally, until the zucchini is tender and flavors have melded together.
6. Add the cooked penne pasta to the skillet with the zucchini and tomato sauce. Toss to coat the pasta in the sauce and let it cook for another 2-3 minutes to allow the flavors to blend.
7. Serve hot, garnished with freshly grated Parmesan cheese and fresh basil leaves, if desired.

Pasta Bucatini
all'Amatriciana

Pasta Bucatini all'Amatriciana

Bucatini all'Amatriciana is a classic Italian pasta dish that originated in Amatrice, a small town in Italy. It's a simple yet flavorful dish that features bucatini pasta tossed in a sauce made with pancetta, tomatoes, onions, red pepper flakes, and Pecorino cheese. The pancetta lends a salty, savory flavor to the sauce, while the red pepper flakes add a hint of heat. The sauce is typically simmered until it thickens and coats the pasta, resulting in a delicious and satisfying meal. Bucatini all'Amatriciana is a popular pasta dish enjoyed by pasta lovers worldwide and is perfect for those who appreciate bold, robust flavors in a quick and easy-to-make meal.

Cooking Information

4
Portions

40
minutes

Medium
Difficulty

450
Calories

Ingredients

- 16 oz (454 g) bucatini pasta
- 4 oz (113 g) pancetta, diced
- 1 small onion, finely chopped
- 2 cloves garlic, minced
- 1/2 tsp red pepper flakes (adjust to taste)
- 1 can (28 oz/800 g) crushed tomatoes
- 1/2 cup (125 ml) red wine
- 1/2 cup (50 g) grated Pecorino cheese
- Salt and pepper, to taste
- Fresh parsley, chopped, for garnish (optional)

Execution

1. Bring a large pot of salted water to a boil. Cook the bucatini pasta according to package instructions until al dente. Drain and set aside.
2. In a large skillet or saucepan, heat the pancetta over medium heat until it starts to render its fat and become crispy. Add the chopped onion and sauté until softened, about 5 minutes.
3. Add the minced garlic and red pepper flakes to the pan and cook for another 1 minute.
4. Stir in the crushed tomatoes and red wine, and bring the sauce to a simmer. Reduce heat to low and let the sauce simmer for about 15-20 minutes, stirring occasionally, until it thickens.
5. Season the sauce with salt and pepper to taste.
6. Add the cooked bucatini pasta to the pan with the sauce and toss to coat the pasta evenly in the sauce.
7. Remove from heat and stir in the grated Pecorino cheese.
8. Serve hot, garnished with chopped fresh parsley, if desired.

Tagliatelle
al Ragu

Tagliatelle al Ragu

Experience the epitome of Italian comfort food with Tagliatelle al Ragu. This timeless dish features al dente tagliatelle pasta dressed in a rich and savory meat sauce. The slow-cooked ragu, made with a medley of tender meats, aromatic herbs, and simmered tomatoes, creates a symphony of flavors that will transport you straight to Italy. Every twirl of the fork captures the essence of homemade goodness and brings a sense of warmth to your palate. Indulge in this classic Italian masterpiece and savor the robust flavors that make Tagliatelle al Ragu a beloved favorite for pasta enthusiasts around the world.

Cooking Information

4
Portions

2
hour total

Medium
Difficulty

500
Calories

Ingredients

- 350g tagliatelle pasta
- 500g ground beef
- 200g pancetta, diced
- 1 onion, finely chopped
- 2 cloves of garlic, minced
- 2 carrots, finely chopped
- 2 celery stalks, finely chopped
- 1 can (400g) crushed tomatoes
- 1 cup beef broth
- 1/2 cup red wine (optional)
- 2 tablespoons tomato paste
- 2 tablespoons olive oil
- 1 teaspoon dried oregano
- 1 teaspoon dried basil
- Salt and pepper to taste
- Grated Parmesan cheese for serving
- Fresh basil leaves for garnish

Execution

1. Heat olive oil in a large saucepan over medium heat. Add pancetta and cook until crispy. Remove pancetta from the pan and set aside.
2. In the same pan, add the ground beef and cook until browned. Add onions, garlic, carrots, and celery. Sauté until vegetables are tender.
3. Return the pancetta to the pan and stir in tomato paste, dried oregano, dried basil, salt, and pepper. Cook for a few minutes to allow the flavors to meld together.
4. Pour in the red wine (if using) and cook until it reduces slightly.
5. Add crushed tomatoes and beef broth to the pan. Stir well and bring to a simmer. Reduce the heat to low, cover, and let the sauce simmer for about 1.5 to 2 hours, stirring occasionally.
6. In a separate pot, bring salted water to a boil. Cook the tagliatelle pasta according to package instructions until al dente. Drain the pasta.
7. Toss the cooked tagliatelle pasta with the ragu sauce until well coated.
8. Serve the Tagliatelle al Ragu hot, garnished with grated Parmesan cheese and fresh basil leaves.
9. Enjoy the rich and hearty flavors of this classic Italian dish, Tagliatelle al Ragu. Bon appétit!

Tortellini
with Pesto Sauce

Tortellini with Pesto Sauce

Tortellini with Pesto Sauce is a delightful Italian pasta dish that combines tender tortellini filled with cheese or meat, tossed in a vibrant and flavorful pesto sauce. This dish is a celebration of fresh ingredients and bold flavors.

The tortellini, with its unique ring-shaped pasta filled with delicious fillings, provides a satisfying bite. The pesto sauce, made from basil, garlic, pine nuts, Parmesan cheese, and olive oil, adds a burst of freshness and herbal aroma to the dish. It's a harmonious marriage of textures and flavors that will please your taste buds.

Whether enjoyed as a main course or a side dish, Tortellini with Pesto Sauce is a versatile and quick option for busy weeknight dinners or special occasions. It's a dish that will transport you to the sunny shores of Italy with every mouthful.

Indulge in the simplicity and elegance of Tortellini with Pesto Sauce, and experience the true essence of Italian cuisine. Buon appetito!

Cooking Information

4
Portions

25
minutes

Easy
Difficulty

500
Calories

Ingredients

- 500g (1 lb) tortellini (cheese or meat-filled)
- 2 cups fresh basil leaves
- 1/3 cup pine nuts
- 2 cloves garlic
- 1/2 cup grated Parmesan cheese
- 1/2 cup extra virgin olive oil
- Salt and pepper to taste

Execution

1. Cook the tortellini according to the package instructions until al dente. Drain and set aside.
2. In a food processor or blender, combine the basil leaves, pine nuts, garlic, and Parmesan cheese. Pulse until finely chopped.
3. While the food processor is running, gradually add the olive oil in a steady stream until a smooth and creamy pesto sauce is formed. Season with salt and pepper to taste.
4. In a large pan, heat the pesto sauce over low heat until warmed through. Add the cooked tortellini to the pan and gently toss to coat the pasta evenly with the sauce.
5. Cook for an additional 2-3 minutes, stirring occasionally, until the tortellini is heated through.
6. Remove from heat and serve the Tortellini with Pesto Sauce immediately. Garnish with additional Parmesan cheese and fresh basil leaves, if desired.

Cannelloni
with Spinach and Ricotta

Cannelloni with Spinach and Ricotta

In this classic Italian dish, delicate pasta tubes, known as cannelloni, are filled with a delicious mixture of spinach and creamy ricotta cheese. The combination of earthy spinach, rich ricotta, and flavorful seasonings creates a mouthwatering filling that is then rolled up in the pasta tubes. The cannelloni are then baked to perfection, resulting in a comforting and satisfying dish that is perfect for a family dinner or special occasion. The creamy ricotta pairs beautifully with the tender spinach, while the pasta provides a satisfying bite. Each mouthful is a delightful balance of flavors and textures. Whether you're a fan of Italian cuisine or simply looking to impress your guests with a homemade pasta dish, Cannelloni with Spinach and Ricotta is sure to be a crowd-pleaser..

Cooking Information

4 Portions

25 minutes

Easy Difficulty

500 Calories

Ingredients

- 12 cannelloni pasta tubes
- 2 cups fresh spinach, chopped
- 1 cup ricotta cheese
- 1/2 cup grated Parmesan cheese
- 1/2 cup shredded mozzarella cheese
- 1 egg, lightly beaten
- 2 cloves garlic, minced
- 1 teaspoon dried oregano
- 1/2 teaspoon salt
- 1/4 teaspoon black pepper
- 2 cups marinara sauce
- Fresh basil leaves, for garnish

Execution

1. Preheat your oven to 375°F (190°C).
2. Cook the cannelloni pasta according to the package instructions. Drain and set aside.
3. In a large bowl, combine the chopped spinach, ricotta cheese, Parmesan cheese, mozzarella cheese, beaten egg, minced garlic, dried oregano, salt, and black pepper. Mix well until all the ingredients are evenly incorporated.
4. Take each cannelloni pasta tube and carefully fill it with the spinach and ricotta mixture using a spoon or piping bag. Place the filled cannelloni in a baking dish, arranging them in a single layer.
5. Pour the marinara sauce over the cannelloni, covering them completely.
6. Cover the baking dish with aluminum foil and bake in the preheated oven for 20 minutes.
7. Remove the foil and bake for an additional 5 minutes, or until the top is golden and bubbly.
8. Remove from the oven and let it cool for a few minutes before serving.
9. Garnish with fresh basil leaves and serve hot.
10. Note: You can serve Cannelloni with Spinach and Ricotta as a main dish accompanied by a side salad or garlic bread for a complete meal. Enjoy the creamy and flavorful combination of spinach and ricotta wrapped in tender pasta tubes!

Maccheroni alla
Chitarra
with Abruzzese Lamb
Ragout

Maccheroni alla Chitarra with Abruzzese Lamb Ragout

Maccheroni alla Chitarra with Abruzzese Lamb Ragout is a classic pasta dish from the Abruzzo region of Italy. The dish features handmade maccheroni pasta, made using a special chitarra pasta cutter, served with a rich and flavorful lamb ragout. The lamb is slowly cooked with aromatic herbs, tomatoes, and red wine, resulting in a tender and savory sauce that coats the pasta perfectly. This dish is a true taste of traditional Italian cuisine, showcasing the rustic flavors of Abruzzo. It's a comforting and satisfying meal that will transport you to the heart of Italy with every bite.

Cooking Information

4 Portions

2 Hour

Medium Difficulty

600 Calories

Ingredients

- 500g maccheroni alla chitarra pasta
- 500g lamb, diced
- 1 onion, finely chopped
- 2 cloves of garlic, minced
- 2 carrots, diced
- 2 celery stalks, diced
- 400g canned crushed tomatoes
- 200ml red wine
- 2 tablespoons tomato paste
- 2 tablespoons olive oil
- 1 teaspoon dried oregano
- 1 teaspoon dried rosemary
- Salt and pepper to taste
- Grated Parmesan cheese, for serving
- Fresh parsley, chopped, for garnish

Execution

1. In a large pot, heat the olive oil over medium heat. Add the diced lamb and cook until browned on all sides. Remove the lamb from the pot and set aside.
2. In the same pot, add the chopped onion, minced garlic, carrots, and celery. Sauté until the vegetables are softened.
3. Return the lamb to the pot and add the crushed tomatoes, tomato paste, red wine, dried oregano, and dried rosemary. Season with salt and pepper to taste. Stir well to combine.
4. Reduce the heat to low and let the lamb ragout simmer for at least 1.5 to 2 hours, stirring occasionally, until the lamb is tender and the flavors are well blended.
5. While the ragout is simmering, cook the maccheroni alla chitarra pasta according to the package instructions until al dente. Drain the pasta.
6. Serve the cooked maccheroni alla chitarra pasta onto individual plates and top with a generous amount of the lamb ragout.
7. Garnish with grated Parmesan cheese and fresh parsley.
8. Serve hot and enjoy this traditional Italian pasta dish.
9. Note: Adjust the seasoning according to your taste preference. You can also sprinkle some red pepper flakes if you prefer a bit of spice.

Spaghetti
alla Nerano

Spaghetti alla Nerano

Spaghetti alla Nerano is a classic Italian pasta dish hailing from the beautiful coastal town of Nerano in the Campania region. This dish is simple yet incredibly flavorful, showcasing the freshness of summer zucchini and the richness of Grana Padano cheese.

Thin spaghetti noodles are tossed with sautéed zucchini, garlic, and a generous amount of grated Grana Padano cheese. The zucchini becomes soft and caramelized, infusing the pasta with its delicate sweetness. The addition of garlic adds a delightful aromatic note, while the cheese brings a creamy and savory element to the dish.

The result is a comforting and satisfying pasta dish that highlights the natural flavors of the ingredients. Spaghetti alla Nerano is perfect for those seeking a light yet delicious meal, reminiscent of sunny Mediterranean flavors.

Note: Adjust the amount of cheese according to your preference, and feel free to sprinkle some freshly chopped basil or parsley on top for a pop of freshness. Enjoy this delightful pasta dish on its own or paired with a crisp salad and a glass of Italian wine for a truly satisfying meal.

Cooking Information

4 Portions

25 minutes

Easy Difficulty

600 Calories

Ingredients

- 12 ounces (340 grams) spaghetti
- 2 medium zucchini
- 3 cloves of garlic, minced
- 1/4 cup extra virgin olive oil
- 1/2 cup grated Grana Padano cheese
- Salt and pepper to taste
- Fresh basil or parsley for garnish (optional)

Execution

1. Bring a large pot of salted water to a boil. Cook the spaghetti according to package instructions until al dente. Drain and set aside.
2. Meanwhile, trim the ends of the zucchini and cut them into thin matchstick-like strips.
3. In a large skillet, heat the olive oil over medium heat. Add the minced garlic and cook until fragrant, about 1 minute.
4. Add the zucchini strips to the skillet and sauté until they become soft and lightly caramelized, about 8-10 minutes.
5. Season the zucchini with salt and pepper to taste.
6. Add the cooked spaghetti to the skillet with the zucchini and toss well to combine, ensuring the pasta is evenly coated with the zucchini and oil.
7. Remove the skillet from heat and sprinkle the grated Grana Padano cheese over the pasta. Toss again to melt the cheese and create a creamy sauce.
8. Serve the Spaghetti alla Nerano hot, garnished with fresh basil or parsley if desired.

Cavatelli
with Sausage and Broccoli Rabe

Cavatelli with Sausage and Broccoli Rabe

Cavatelli with Sausage and Broccoli Rabe is a classic Italian pasta dish that combines hearty flavors and vibrant greens. The tender cavatelli pasta pairs perfectly with the savory sausage and the slightly bitter broccoli rabe. This recipe is a delightful balance of textures and tastes, making it a satisfying meal for any occasion.

In this dish, the sausage is cooked until browned and flavorful, while the broccoli rabe is blanched to retain its vibrant green color and crispness. The cavatelli pasta is then tossed with the sausage and broccoli rabe, creating a harmonious blend of ingredients.

The combination of the rich sausage, the earthy bitterness of the broccoli rabe, and the al dente pasta creates a truly comforting and satisfying dish. Whether enjoyed as a weeknight dinner or served for special occasions, Cavatelli with Sausage and Broccoli Rabe is sure to impress with its bold flavors and delightful textures.

Cooking Information

4 Portions

40 minutes

Medium Difficulty

500 Calories

Ingredients

- 1 pound cavatelli pasta
- 1 pound Italian sausage, casings removed
- 1 bunch broccoli rabe, trimmed and cut into bite-sized pieces
- 3 cloves garlic, minced
- ¼ teaspoon red pepper flakes (adjust to taste)
- ½ cup grated Parmesan cheese
- 2 tablespoons olive oil
- Salt and pepper to taste

Execution

1. Bring a large pot of salted water to a boil. Cook the cavatelli pasta according to package instructions until al dente. Drain and set aside.
2. In a large skillet, heat olive oil over medium heat. Add the sausage and cook, breaking it up with a wooden spoon, until browned and cooked through.
3. Add the minced garlic and red pepper flakes to the skillet and cook for an additional minute until fragrant.
4. Add the broccoli rabe to the skillet and sauté until wilted and tender, about 5-7 minutes. Season with salt and pepper to taste.
5. Add the cooked cavatelli pasta to the skillet with the sausage and broccoli rabe. Toss well to combine and heat through.
6. Remove from heat and sprinkle with grated Parmesan cheese. Stir until the cheese is melted and coats the pasta.
7. Serve hot and enjoy!

Fusilli alla Caprese

Fusilli alla Caprese

Fusilli alla Caprese is a delightful pasta dish that combines cooked fusilli with fresh tomatoes, mozzarella, basil, and a drizzle of olive oil. This classic Italian recipe captures the flavors of Caprese salad in a light and refreshing way. It's the perfect choice for a quick and satisfying meal that celebrates the essence of Mediterranean cuisine.

Cooking Information

4 Portions

10 minutes

Easy Difficulty

450 Calories

Ingredients

- 12 ounces (340 grams) of fusilli pasta
- 2 cups cherry tomatoes, halved
- 8 ounces (225 grams) fresh mozzarella, diced
- 1/2 cup fresh basil leaves, torn
- 3 tablespoons extra-virgin olive oil
- Salt and pepper to taste

Execution

1. Cook the fusilli pasta according to the package instructions until al dente. Drain and set aside.
2. In a large mixing bowl, combine the cooked fusilli, cherry tomatoes, mozzarella, and torn basil leaves.
3. Drizzle the extra-virgin olive oil over the pasta mixture and toss gently to coat.
4. Season with salt and pepper to taste.
5. Allow the flavors to meld together for a few minutes before serving.
6. Serve the Fusilli alla Caprese warm or at room temperature.
7. Optionally, garnish with additional torn basil leaves before serving.

Pesto Genovese
with Trofie

Pesto Genovese with Trofie

Pesto Genovese with Trofie is a classic Italian pasta dish that originates from the region of Liguria. This flavorful recipe combines homemade pesto sauce with trofie pasta, resulting in a delicious and aromatic dish.

The vibrant green pesto is made from fresh basil leaves, pine nuts, garlic, Parmesan cheese, and extra-virgin olive oil. It offers a perfect balance of flavors, with the basil providing a refreshing herbal note, the pine nuts adding a subtle crunch, and the Parmesan lending a savory richness.

Trofie, a traditional pasta shape from Liguria, is the perfect choice for this dish. Its twisted and elongated shape allows the pesto sauce to cling to every bite, ensuring that each mouthful is packed with flavor.

This recipe is incredibly versatile and can be enjoyed as a main course or served as a side dish. It's quick and easy to prepare, making it a great option for busy weeknight dinners or when you're craving a taste of Italy.

Whether you're a seasoned cook or a pasta enthusiast, Pesto Genovese with Trofie is sure to impress your taste buds and transport you to the beautiful coastal region of Liguria.

Cooking Information

4
Portions

15
minutes

Easy
Difficulty

450
Calories

Ingredients

- 12 ounces (340 grams) trofie pasta
- 2 cups fresh basil leaves
- 1/3 cup pine nuts
- 2 cloves garlic, minced
- 1/2 cup grated Parmesan cheese
- 1/2 cup extra-virgin olive oil
- Salt, to taste
- Freshly ground black pepper, to taste

Execution

1. Bring a large pot of salted water to a boil. Add the trofie pasta and cook according to the package instructions until al dente. Drain the pasta and set aside.
2. In a food processor or blender, combine the basil leaves, pine nuts, minced garlic, and grated Parmesan cheese. Pulse until the ingredients are finely chopped.
3. With the food processor or blender running, gradually add the extra-virgin olive oil in a steady stream until the mixture forms a smooth and creamy pesto sauce.
4. Season the pesto sauce with salt and freshly ground black pepper to taste. Adjust the seasoning as needed.
5. In a large serving bowl, toss the cooked trofie pasta with the pesto sauce until well coated.
6. Serve the Pesto Genovese with Trofie warm or at room temperature. Optionally, garnish with additional grated Parmesan cheese and a sprinkle of fresh basil leaves.
7. Enjoy!
8. Note: You can customize this dish by adding cherry tomatoes, sliced black olives, or cooked shrimp for extra flavor and texture.
9. Enjoy the delightful flavors of this traditional Ligurian dish, Pesto Genovese with Trofie. Buon appetito!

Tortellini
in Brodo

Tortellini in Brodo

Indulge in the heartwarming flavors of Tortellini in Brodo, a beloved Italian dish that brings comfort and satisfaction to every spoonful. This traditional recipe features delicate, handmade tortellini nestled in a rich, savory broth, creating a perfect harmony of flavors.

The tender pasta pockets are typically filled with a combination of meat, cheese, or vegetables, adding a burst of flavor with every bite. As you savor the comforting warmth of the broth, the tortellini release their delightful essence, making each spoonful a delight to the palate.

Tortellini in Brodo is not only a delicious dish but also a symbol of Italian culinary tradition and family gatherings. It is often enjoyed during festive occasions or as a comforting meal on a chilly evening. With its simplicity and timeless appeal, it has become a staple in Italian households and a favorite in Italian restaurants around the world.

Whether you prepare the tortellini from scratch or opt for store-bought varieties, Tortellini in Brodo is a dish that embodies the essence of Italian cuisine – simple, flavorful, and comforting. It is a testament to the beauty of combining humble ingredients to create a dish that brings joy and warmth to the table.

Experience the comforting embrace of Tortellini in Brodo and let its flavors transport you to the heart of Italy.

Cooking Information

4
Portions

35
minutes

Easy
Difficulty

500
Calories

Ingredients

- 1 pound (450g) tortellini (meat, cheese, or vegetable-filled)
- 8 cups (2 liters) chicken or vegetable broth
- 1 medium-sized onion, finely chopped
- 2 cloves of garlic, minced
- 2 tablespoons olive oil
- 1 bay leaf
- Salt and pepper to taste
- Fresh parsley, chopped (for garnish)
- Grated Parmesan cheese (optional, for serving)

Execution

1. In a large pot, heat olive oil over medium heat. Add the chopped onion and minced garlic, and sauté until translucent and fragrant.
2. Pour in the chicken or vegetable broth and add the bay leaf. Bring the broth to a simmer.
3. Carefully drop the tortellini into the simmering broth and cook according to the package instructions or until the tortellini are tender.
4. Once the tortellini are cooked, remove the pot from heat and season with salt and pepper to taste.
5. Ladle the Tortellini in Brodo into individual serving bowls, ensuring each bowl has a generous amount of tortellini and broth.
6. Garnish with freshly chopped parsley and, if desired, sprinkle with grated Parmesan cheese.
7. Serve hot and enjoy this comforting bowl of Tortellini in Brodo.
8. Note: You can customize this recipe by adding vegetables such as spinach or carrots to the broth, or by using different types of tortellini fillings to suit your taste preferences.

Farfalle
al Salmone

Farfalle al Salmone

Farfalle al Salmone is a delightful Italian pasta dish that combines tender farfalle pasta with succulent salmon in a creamy and flavorful sauce. This dish is a harmonious blend of the richness of the salmon, the creaminess of the sauce, and the satisfying texture of the farfalle pasta. It's a perfect choice for seafood lovers looking for a comforting and elegant meal.

Cooking Information

2 Portions

30 Minutes

Medium Difficulty

600 Calories

Ingredients

- 8 ounces (225g) farfalle pasta
- 8 ounces (225g) fresh salmon fillet, skin removed
- 2 tablespoons olive oil
- 2 cloves of garlic, minced
- 1 cup (240ml) heavy cream
- 1/4 cup (60ml) chicken or vegetable broth
- 1/4 cup (60ml) dry white wine (optional)
- 1/4 cup (30g) grated Parmesan cheese
- 2 tablespoons fresh dill, chopped
- Salt and pepper to taste
- Lemon wedges (for serving)

Execution

1. Cook the farfalle pasta according to the package instructions until al dente. Drain and set aside.
2. Cut the salmon fillet into small bite-sized pieces.
3. In a large skillet, heat the olive oil over medium heat. Add the minced garlic and sauté until fragrant, about 1-2 minutes.
4. Add the salmon pieces to the skillet and cook until they are lightly browned and cooked through, about 3-4 minutes per side. Remove the salmon from the skillet and set aside.
5. In the same skillet, pour in the heavy cream, chicken or vegetable broth, and dry white wine (if using). Bring the mixture to a simmer and let it cook for about 5 minutes, stirring occasionally.
6. Stir in the grated Parmesan cheese until it is melted and incorporated into the sauce.
7. Add the cooked farfalle pasta and cooked salmon back to the skillet. Gently toss to coat the pasta and salmon with the creamy sauce.
8. Season with salt and pepper to taste, and sprinkle the chopped dill over the pasta.
9. Remove from heat and divide the Farfalle al Salmone into individual serving plates or bowls.
10. Serve hot, garnished with lemon wedges for a refreshing touch.
11. Note: Feel free to add additional ingredients like cherry tomatoes or steamed vegetables to the dish to add more flavor and color. Adjust the seasoning and sauce consistency according to your taste preference.

Spaghetti

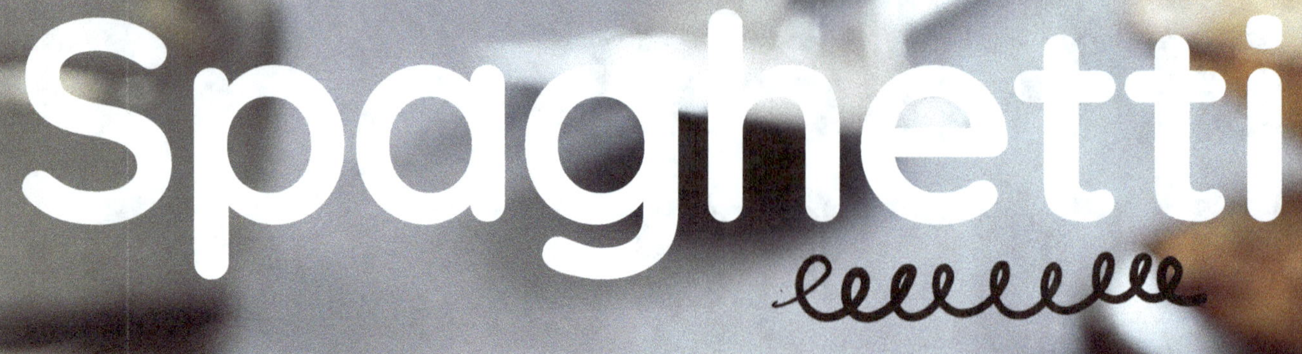

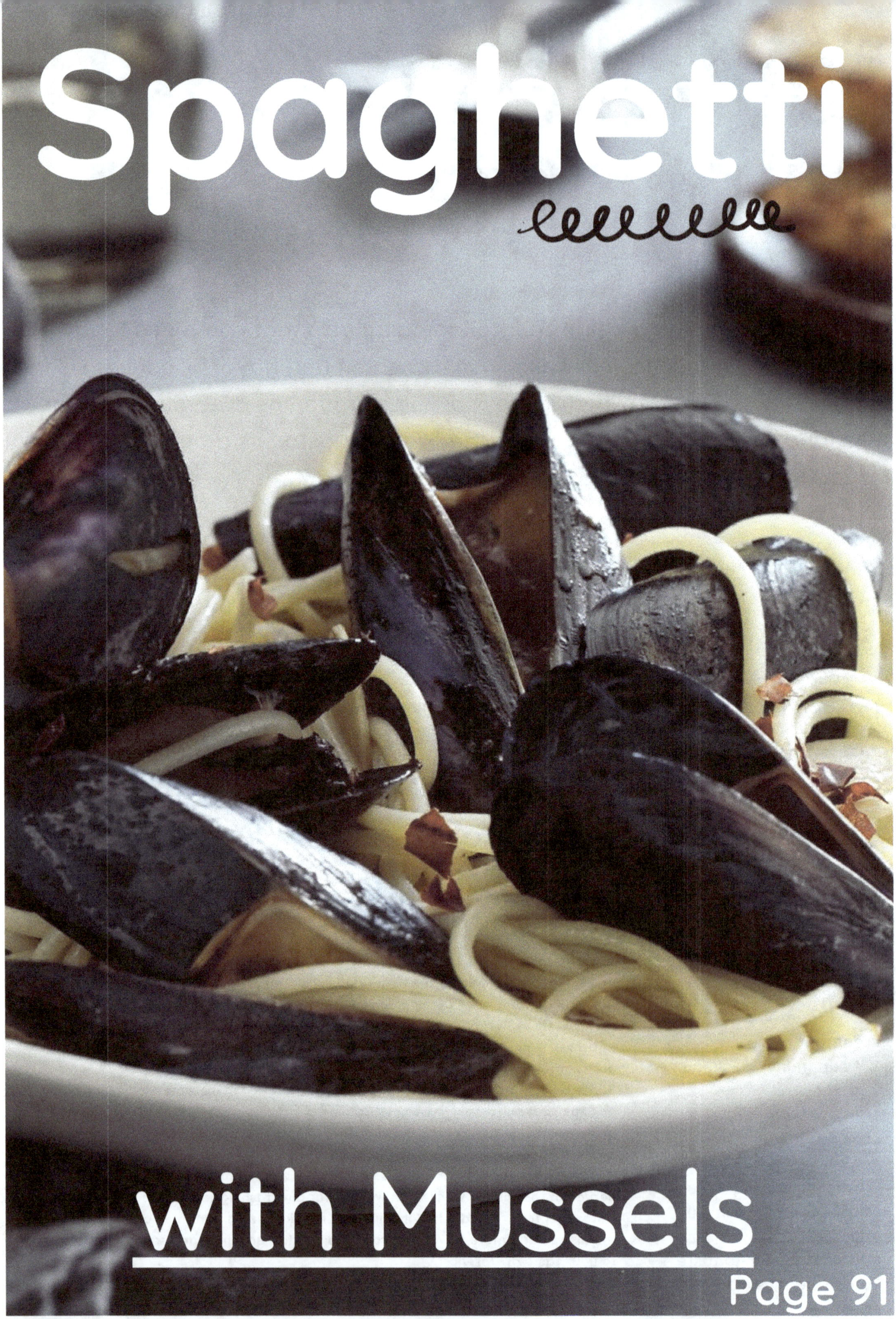

with Mussels

Page 91

Spaghetti with Mussels

Spaghetti with Mussels is a classic Italian pasta dish that showcases the delightful combination of tender spaghetti noodles and fresh, briny mussels. This dish is a celebration of the sea, with the flavors of the ocean infused into every bite. The spaghetti absorbs the rich flavors of the tomato-based sauce, while the mussels add a touch of sweetness and a hint of the sea. It's a satisfying and impressive dish that will transport you to the coastal shores of Italy.

Cooking Information

2
Portions

35
Minutes

Medium
Difficulty

600
Calories

Ingredients

- 8 ounces (225g) spaghetti
- 2 pounds (900g) fresh mussels, cleaned and debearded
- 2 tablespoons olive oil
- 4 cloves of garlic, minced
- 1 small onion, finely chopped
- 1 cup (240ml) crushed tomatoes
- 1/2 cup (120ml) dry white wine
- 1/4 teaspoon red pepper flakes (adjust to taste)
- Salt and pepper to taste
- Fresh parsley, chopped (for garnish)

Execution

1. Cook the spaghetti in a large pot of salted boiling water until al dente. Drain and set aside.
2. In a separate large pot, heat the olive oil over medium heat. Add the minced garlic and chopped onion, and sauté until fragrant and softened, about 2-3 minutes.
3. Add the crushed tomatoes, dry white wine, and red pepper flakes to the pot. Season with salt and pepper to taste. Stir to combine and let the sauce simmer for about 10 minutes to allow the flavors to meld together.
4. Add the cleaned mussels to the pot, cover with a lid, and cook for about 5-7 minutes, or until the mussels have opened. Discard any mussels that do not open.
5. Remove the cooked mussels from the pot and set them aside, keeping them warm.
6. Add the cooked spaghetti to the pot with the tomato sauce, tossing it gently to coat the pasta with the sauce.
7. Divide the spaghetti with mussels into individual serving plates or bowls. Top each portion with some of the cooked mussels.
8. Garnish with fresh chopped parsley for a burst of freshness and color.
9. Serve immediately while still hot and enjoy the delightful flavors of the sea-infused spaghetti.
10. Note: You can customize the dish by adding additional ingredients such as chopped tomatoes, olives, or fresh herbs to enhance the flavors. Adjust the level of spiciness by increasing or decreasing the amount of red pepper flakes.

Pappardelle
with Wild Boar Sauce

Pappardelle with Wild Boar Sauce

Pappardelle with Wild Boar Sauce is a hearty and flavorsome Italian pasta dish that combines wide, ribbon-like pappardelle noodles with a rich and savory wild boar sauce. The tender and succulent wild boar meat is slow-cooked with aromatic herbs, vegetables, and tomatoes, creating a luscious sauce that coats the pappardelle beautifully. This dish offers a rustic and indulgent dining experience, with the robust flavors of the wild boar melding perfectly with the pasta. It's a true delight for pasta and meat lovers alike.

Cooking Information

2 Portions

2 hours 15 minutes

Medium Difficulty

600 Calories

Ingredients

- 8 ounces (225g) pappardelle pasta
- 1 pound (450g) wild boar meat, diced (substitute with pork if unavailable)
- 2 tablespoons olive oil
- 1 onion, finely chopped
- 2 cloves of garlic, minced
- 1 carrot, finely chopped
- 1 celery stalk, finely chopped
- 1 cup (240ml) crushed tomatoes
- 1 cup (240ml) red wine
- 1 cup (240ml) beef or vegetable broth
- 2 sprigs fresh rosemary
- 2 bay leaves
- Salt and pepper to taste
- Grated Parmesan cheese (for garnish)
- Fresh parsley, chopped (for garnish)

Execution

1. In a large pot or Dutch oven, heat the olive oil over medium heat. Add the diced wild boar meat and cook until browned on all sides. Remove the meat from the pot and set it aside.
2. In the same pot, add the chopped onion, minced garlic, carrot, and celery. Sauté until the vegetables have softened and are slightly caramelized, about 5-7 minutes.
3. Return the browned wild boar meat to the pot and add the crushed tomatoes, red wine, beef or vegetable broth, fresh rosemary sprigs, and bay leaves. Season with salt and pepper to taste. Stir to combine all the ingredients.
4. Bring the sauce to a simmer, then reduce the heat to low. Cover the pot partially with a lid and let it cook slowly for about 2 hours, or until the wild boar meat is tender and the flavors have melded together.
5. While the sauce is simmering, cook the pappardelle pasta in a large pot of salted boiling water until al dente. Drain the pasta and set it aside.
6. Remove the rosemary sprigs and bay leaves from the sauce.
7. Add the cooked pappardelle pasta to the pot with the wild boar sauce, tossing gently to coat the noodles with the rich sauce.
8. Divide the pappardelle with wild boar sauce into individual serving plates or bowls.
9. Garnish with grated Parmesan cheese and freshly chopped parsley for an added layer of flavor and visual appeal.
10. Serve immediately and savor the delectable combination of tender pappardelle noodles and the robust, savory wild boar sauce.
11. Note: You can enhance the flavors of the sauce by adding a dash of red pepper flakes for a hint of spiciness. Feel free to adjust the seasoning and ingredients according to your taste preferences. Enjoy this satisfying and comforting dish, perfect for a special occasion or a cozy meal at home.

Trapanese
Pesto Pasta

Trapanese Pesto Pasta

Trapanese Pesto Pasta is a vibrant and aromatic Italian dish that originates from the region of Sicily. This unique twist on traditional pesto features a delicious blend of sun-dried tomatoes, fresh basil, garlic, almonds, and pecorino cheese. Tossed with al dente pasta, it creates a flavorful and satisfying meal that celebrates the vibrant flavors of the Mediterranean. Trapanese Pesto Pasta is a true crowd-pleaser, perfect for both casual weeknight dinners and special occasions

Cooking Information

4-6 Portions

30 Minutes

Easy Difficulty

275 Calories

Ingredients

- 8 ounces (225g) spaghetti or your preferred pasta
- 1 cup (150g) sun-dried tomatoes (packed in oil), drained
- 1 cup (30g) fresh basil leaves
- 1/2 cup (60g) almonds
- 2 cloves of garlic
- 1/4 cup (30g) grated pecorino cheese
- 1/4 cup (60ml) extra virgin olive oil
- Salt and pepper to taste
- Fresh basil leaves (for garnish)

Execution

1. Bring a large pot of salted water to a boil. Cook the spaghetti according to package instructions until al dente. Drain and set aside.
2. In a food processor or blender, combine the sun-dried tomatoes, fresh basil leaves, almonds, garlic, grated pecorino cheese, and a pinch of salt and pepper.
3. Pulse the ingredients until they form a coarse paste.
4. While the food processor is running, slowly drizzle in the extra virgin olive oil until the pesto becomes smooth and well combined. Adjust the consistency by adding more olive oil if needed.
5. In a large pan, heat a drizzle of olive oil over medium heat. Add the prepared pesto to the pan and cook for a couple of minutes, stirring occasionally.
6. Add the cooked spaghetti to the pan with the pesto sauce. Toss the pasta gently until it is well coated with the sauce and heated through.
7. Season with additional salt and pepper to taste, if desired.
8. Divide the Trapanese Pesto Pasta into individual serving plates or bowls.
9. Garnish with fresh basil leaves for an extra touch of freshness and presentation.
10. Serve immediately and enjoy the delightful combination of the rich, tangy sun-dried tomato pesto and the al dente spaghetti.
11. Note: Feel free to customize the recipe by adding your favorite ingredients such as olives, cherry tomatoes, or cooked shrimp for added flavor and variety. Experiment with different types of pasta to find your preferred combination. This Trapanese Pesto Pasta is sure to impress your guests with its vibrant colors and exquisite taste.

Fettuccine
with Shrimp and Asparagus

Fettuccine with Shrimp and Asparagus

Fettuccine with Shrimp and Asparagus is a delightful pasta dish that combines the succulent flavors of shrimp with the freshness of asparagus. The tender shrimp and crisp asparagus are tossed in a creamy sauce and served over al dente fettuccine noodles. This dish is a perfect balance of flavors and textures, making it a wonderful choice for a satisfying meal. Whether you're preparing a special dinner for guests or simply treating yourself to a delicious pasta dish, Fettuccine with Shrimp and Asparagus is sure to impress with its vibrant colors and mouthwatering taste.

Cooking Information

4 Portions

30 Minutes

Medium Difficulty

380 Calories

Ingredients

- 8 ounces fettuccine pasta
- 1 pound large shrimp, peeled and deveined
- 1 bunch asparagus, trimmed and cut into bite-sized pieces
- 2 tablespoons olive oil
- 3 cloves garlic, minced
- 1/2 cup chicken broth
- 1/2 cup heavy cream
- 1/2 cup grated Parmesan cheese
- Salt and pepper to taste
- Fresh parsley, chopped (for garnish)

Execution

1. Cook the fettuccine pasta according to package instructions. Drain and set aside.
2. In a large skillet, heat olive oil over medium heat. Add minced garlic and sauté until fragrant.
3. Add shrimp to the skillet and cook until pink and opaque, about 2-3 minutes per side. Remove the shrimp from the skillet and set aside.
4. In the same skillet, add the asparagus and cook until tender-crisp, about 3-4 minutes.
5. Pour in the chicken broth and bring to a simmer. Let it cook for 2 minutes.
6. Stir in the heavy cream and grated Parmesan cheese. Cook until the sauce thickens, about 2-3 minutes.
7. Season the sauce with salt and pepper to taste.
8. Add the cooked fettuccine to the skillet and toss well to coat the pasta in the sauce.
9. Return the cooked shrimp to the skillet and gently toss to combine.
10. Remove from heat and garnish with chopped parsley.
11. Serve hot and enjoy!

Spaghetti
with Artichokes and Tomatoes

Spaghetti with Artichokes and Tomatoes

Spaghetti with Artichokes and Tomatoes is a delightful pasta dish that brings together the vibrant flavors of fresh artichokes and juicy tomatoes. This classic Italian recipe is a celebration of simplicity and balance. The tender spaghetti noodles perfectly complement the tender artichoke hearts and the bright acidity of the tomatoes. The dish is finished off with a touch of garlic, fragrant herbs, and a sprinkle of grated Parmesan cheese.

This light and refreshing pasta dish is sure to impress with its beautiful presentation and satisfying flavors. It's an excellent choice for both casual weeknight dinners and special occasions. Whether you're a pasta enthusiast or simply appreciate the taste of Mediterranean-inspired cuisine, Spaghetti with Artichokes and Tomatoes is a must-try recipe that will transport you to the sunny flavors of Italy.

Cooking Information

4 Portions

30 Minutes

Easy Difficulty

350 Calories

Ingredients

- 8 ounces (225 grams) spaghetti
- 2 tablespoons olive oil
- 2 cloves garlic, minced
- 1 can (14 ounces) artichoke hearts, drained and quartered
- 1 can (14 ounces) diced tomatoes
- 1 teaspoon dried oregano
- Salt and pepper to taste
- Fresh basil leaves, for garnish
- Grated Parmesan cheese, for serving

Execution

1. Cook the spaghetti according to package instructions until al dente. Drain and set aside.
2. In a large skillet, heat the olive oil over medium heat. Add the minced garlic and sauté for about 1 minute until fragrant.
3. Add the artichoke hearts to the skillet and cook for 2-3 minutes until lightly browned.
4. Stir in the diced tomatoes and dried oregano. Season with salt and pepper to taste. Cook for another 5 minutes, allowing the flavors to blend together.
5. Add the cooked spaghetti to the skillet and toss gently to coat the pasta with the sauce.
6. Divide the spaghetti with artichokes and tomatoes among four plates. Garnish with fresh basil leaves.
7. Serve hot, sprinkled with grated Parmesan cheese.

Spaghetti
with Tuna and Tomato
Sauce

Spaghetti with Tuna and Tomato Sauce

Spaghetti with Tuna and Tomato Sauce is a delightful Italian pasta dish that combines the rich flavors of tuna and tangy tomato sauce. This classic recipe is perfect for seafood lovers and those seeking a quick and satisfying meal. The tender spaghetti noodles are tossed in a savory tomato sauce infused with garlic, onions, and herbs, while the flaked tuna adds a touch of brininess and protein. With its balance of flavors and simplicity, Spaghetti with Tuna and Tomato Sauce is a go-to choice for a delicious and wholesome pasta dinner.

Cooking Information

4
Portions

20
Minutes

Easy
Difficulty

400
Calories

Ingredients

- 12 oz (340g) spaghetti
- 2 tbsp olive oil
- 1 small onion, finely chopped
- 2 cloves garlic, minced
- 1 can (14 oz/400g) diced tomatoes
- 1 can (5 oz/140g) tuna in olive oil, drained and flaked
- 1/2 tsp dried oregano
- 1/4 tsp red pepper flakes (optional)
- Salt and black pepper, to taste
- Fresh basil leaves, for garnish

Execution

1. Cook the spaghetti according to the package instructions until al dente. Drain and set aside.
2. In a large skillet, heat the olive oil over medium heat. Add the chopped onion and minced garlic, and sauté until fragrant and golden.
3. Add the diced tomatoes to the skillet and cook for about 5 minutes, allowing the flavors to meld together.
4. Stir in the flaked tuna, dried oregano, and red pepper flakes (if using). Season with salt and black pepper to taste. Simmer for another 5 minutes.
5. Add the cooked spaghetti to the skillet and toss well to coat the noodles with the sauce. Cook for an additional 2-3 minutes, allowing the flavors to meld together.
6. Serve the Spaghetti with Tuna and Tomato Sauce hot, garnished with fresh basil leaves.

Pumpkin Ravioli
with Sage Butter Sauce

Pumpkin Ravioli with Sage Butter Sauce

Indulge in the delightful flavors of Pumpkin Ravioli with Sage Butter Sauce. This classic Italian dish combines tender homemade ravioli filled with a creamy pumpkin and cheese mixture, served with a velvety sage-infused butter sauce. The earthy sweetness of the pumpkin, combined with the aromatic sage and rich butter, creates a perfect balance of flavors that will tantalize your taste buds. Whether you're celebrating a special occasion or simply craving a comforting pasta dish, Pumpkin Ravioli with Sage Butter Sauce is sure to impress.

Cooking Information

4 Portions

1 Hour

Medium Difficulty

400 Calories

Ingredients

- 1 package (about 24 ounces) of fresh or store-bought pumpkin ravioli
- 4 tablespoons unsalted butter
- 8-10 fresh sage leaves
- 1/4 cup grated Parmesan cheese
- Salt and pepper to taste

Execution

1. Bring a large pot of salted water to a boil and cook the pumpkin ravioli according to the package instructions until al dente. Drain and set aside.
2. In a large skillet, melt the butter over medium heat. Add the sage leaves and cook until crispy, about 2-3 minutes. Remove the sage leaves and set them aside for garnish.
3. Continue cooking the butter until it turns a light golden brown color, being careful not to burn it.
4. Add the cooked ravioli to the skillet and gently toss them in the sage-infused butter sauce until well coated. Cook for an additional 1-2 minutes to heat through.
5. Season with salt and pepper to taste.
6. Serve the pumpkin ravioli on individual plates, garnishing each portion with the crispy sage leaves and a sprinkle of grated Parmesan cheese.
7. Enjoy the delicious Pumpkin Ravioli with Sage Butter Sauce immediately while it's still hot.

Florentine
Cannelloni

Florentine Cannelloni

Florentine Cannelloni is a classic Italian dish that features delicate pasta tubes filled with a rich and flavorful mixture of spinach and ricotta cheese. The cannelloni are then baked in a luscious tomato and béchamel sauce, resulting in a deliciously satisfying meal. This dish showcases the essence of Italian comfort food, combining creamy cheese, vibrant spinach, and hearty tomato flavors. With its enticing aroma and enticing presentation, Florentine Cannelloni is sure to impress both family and guests. Whether served as a main course or part of a larger Italian feast, this dish is a true delight for pasta lovers everywhere.

Cooking Information

4 Portions

1 Hour

Medium Difficulty

400 Calories

Ingredients

- 12 cannelloni tubes
- 10 oz spinach, cooked and drained
- 1 cup ricotta cheese
- 1/2 cup grated Parmesan cheese
- 1 egg, beaten
- 1/2 teaspoon dried oregano
- 1/2 teaspoon garlic powder
- Salt and pepper to taste
- 2 cups tomato sauce
- 1 cup béchamel sauce
- 1/4 cup grated mozzarella cheese

Execution

1. Cook the cannelloni tubes according to the package instructions. Drain and set aside.
2. In a mixing bowl, combine the cooked spinach, ricotta cheese, grated Parmesan cheese, beaten egg, dried oregano, garlic powder, salt, and pepper. Mix well to form a creamy filling.
3. Preheat the oven to 350°F (175°C).
4. Spoon the spinach and ricotta mixture into a piping bag or a resealable plastic bag with the corner snipped off.
5. Fill each cannelloni tube with the spinach and ricotta mixture using the piping bag, or simply use a spoon to carefully stuff the tubes.
6. Spread a thin layer of tomato sauce on the bottom of a baking dish.
7. Arrange the filled cannelloni tubes in a single layer on top of the tomato sauce.
8. Pour the remaining tomato sauce over the cannelloni, making sure they are evenly coated.
9. Drizzle the béchamel sauce over the tomato sauce.
10. Sprinkle the grated mozzarella cheese on top.
11. Cover the baking dish with aluminum foil and bake in the preheated oven for 30 minutes.
12. Remove the foil and continue baking for an additional 10-15 minutes, or until the cheese is melted and golden.
13. Remove from the oven and let it cool for a few minutes before serving.
14. Serve the Florentine Cannelloni hot, garnished with fresh basil or parsley if desired.
15. Note: You can prepare the cannelloni in advance and refrigerate them before baking. Just make sure to adjust the baking time accordingly.
16. Enjoy the rich and comforting flavors of Florentine Cannelloni, a delightful Italian pasta dish that will satisfy your taste buds and leave you craving for more.

Ricotta
and Spinach Ravioli

Ricotta and Spinach Ravioli

Ricotta and Spinach Ravioli is a classic Italian pasta dish that combines the delicate flavors of creamy ricotta cheese and earthy spinach. The homemade pasta dough is filled with a mixture of fresh ricotta, wilted spinach, Parmesan cheese, and aromatic herbs. The ravioli are carefully sealed and cooked until tender, resulting in pockets of goodness ready to be enjoyed. Served with a drizzle of olive oil and a sprinkle of Parmesan, these ravioli are a comforting and satisfying dish. Whether you're a pasta aficionado or simply looking to savor authentic Italian flavors, Ricotta and Spinach Ravioli is sure to impress your taste buds.

Cooking Information

4 Portions

1 Hour

Medium Difficulty

450 Calories

Ingredients

- 10.5 oz fresh spinach
- 8.8 oz ricotta cheese
- 1.8 oz Parmesan cheese, grated
- 1 egg
- ½ teaspoon nutmeg, freshly grated
- Salt and pepper to taste
- 10.5 oz all-purpose flour
- 3 large eggs
- Water, for sealing the ravioli
- Olive oil, for drizzling
- Extra Parmesan cheese, for serving

Execution

1. Start by preparing the filling. Wash the spinach thoroughly and blanch it in boiling water for 1-2 minutes. Drain and squeeze out any excess water. Finely chop the cooked spinach.
2. In a mixing bowl, combine the chopped spinach, ricotta cheese, grated Parmesan, egg, nutmeg, salt, and pepper. Mix well until all the ingredients are evenly incorporated.
3. In a separate large bowl, place the flour and make a well in the center. Crack the eggs into the well and gradually incorporate the flour into the eggs using a fork or your hands. Knead the dough until it becomes smooth and elastic.
4. Divide the dough into smaller portions and roll each portion into a thin sheet using a pasta machine or a rolling pin. The sheets should be about 1/8 inch thick.
5. Spoon small dollops of the ricotta and spinach filling onto one half of the pasta sheet, leaving enough space between each dollop. Fold the other half of the sheet over the filling.
6. Use your fingers to gently press around each mound of filling, sealing the edges of the ravioli. Cut the ravioli into individual pieces using a sharp knife or a fluted pastry wheel.
7. Bring a large pot of salted water to a boil. Add the ravioli and cook them for about 5 minutes or until they float to the surface. Be careful not to overcrowd the pot; cook them in batches if necessary.
8. Once cooked, drain the ravioli and transfer them to a serving dish. Drizzle with a little olive oil and sprinkle with extra grated Parmesan cheese.
9. Serve the ricotta and spinach ravioli hot, garnished with fresh herbs if desired. Enjoy!

Agnolotti
del Plin

Agnolotti del Plin

Agnolotti del Plin is a traditional Italian pasta dish hailing from the Piedmont region. This delectable recipe features small pockets of pasta filled with a savory mixture of ground meat, spinach, onions, garlic, and parsley. The pasta is carefully sealed to create a delightful triangular shape. Cooked to perfection, these agnolotti are tender and bursting with flavor. Served with a sprinkle of grated Parmesan cheese, they are a true delight for pasta lovers. Agnolotti del Plin is a labor of love, requiring a bit of skill to assemble, but the result is well worth the effort. Enjoy this classic Italian dish that showcases the rich culinary heritage of the Piedmont region.

Cooking Information

 4-6 Portions

 1 Hour

 Medium Difficulty

 400 Calories

Ingredients

- 200g all-purpose flour
- 2 large eggs
- 200g ground meat (e.g., beef, pork, or a combination)
- 100g cooked spinach, squeezed dry and finely chopped
- 1 small onion, finely chopped
- 1 clove garlic, minced
- 1 tablespoon fresh parsley, finely chopped
- Salt and pepper to taste
- Egg wash (1 egg beaten with a splash of water)
- Grated Parmesan cheese, for serving
- Butter or olive oil, for sautéing

Execution

1. In a large mixing bowl, combine the flour and eggs. Mix until a dough forms. Knead the dough on a lightly floured surface for about 5 minutes until it becomes smooth and elastic. Cover the dough with a clean kitchen towel and let it rest for 30 minutes.
2. Meanwhile, in a separate bowl, combine the ground meat, chopped spinach, onion, garlic, and parsley. Season with salt and pepper. Mix well until all the ingredients are evenly incorporated.
3. Roll out the pasta dough into a thin sheet using a rolling pin or pasta machine. Cut the dough into small squares, about 2 inches in size.
4. Place a small amount of the meat filling in the center of each square. Fold the dough over the filling to form a triangle. Press the edges together to seal the agnolotti, making sure there are no air pockets.
5. Bring a large pot of salted water to a boil. Carefully add the agnolotti and cook them for about 5-7 minutes or until they float to the surface. Remove them from the water using a slotted spoon and set them aside.
6. In a separate pan, melt butter or heat olive oil over medium heat. Add the cooked agnolotti to the pan and sauté them for a few minutes until they are lightly browned.
7. Serve the agnolotti del Plin hot, sprinkled with grated Parmesan cheese. They can be enjoyed on their own or with a light sauce of your choice.

her exquisite culinary skills and unwavering love for Italian cuisine, Chef Mary was on a mission to preserve the authenticity of traditional pasta recipes.

Growing up in a small village surrounded by lush olive groves and vineyards, Chef Mary was immersed in the rich culinary heritage of Italy from an early age. She spent countless hours in her Nonna's kitchen, learning the secrets of making pasta from scratch and savoring the flavors of homemade sauces passed down through generations.

As Chef Mary's culinary prowess blossomed, she felt a deep calling to share her knowledge and passion with the world. She embarked on a journey to uncover the hidden gems of Italian pasta, venturing to different regions, conversing with local nonnas, and tasting the diverse flavors that each place had to offer.

With every recipe she discovered, Chef Mary could feel the heartbeat of Italy pulsating through her. The vibrant colors of fresh tomatoes, the aroma of basil and garlic, and the delicate texture of handmade pasta all became a part of her culinary identity.

Driven by her desire to preserve the authenticity of Italian pasta, Chef Mary diligently curated a collection of recipes that captured the essence of each region she had explored. From the iconic spaghetti alle vongole of the coastal regions to the hearty rigatoni alla amatriciana from Rome, each dish was a testament to the rich tapestry of flavors that Italy had to offer.

In her book, "Authentic Italian Pasta Recipes," Chef Mary not only shared these cherished recipes but also delved into the stories and traditions behind them. She believed that food was a powerful medium for connecting people and bridging cultures, and she wanted her readers to experience the same joy and connection she felt with every bite.

As the pages of her book came to life, Chef Mary envisioned families gathered around the dinner table, savoring the flavors of Italy, and creating memories that would last a lifetime. She hoped that her recipes would inspire home cooks to embrace the art of pasta-making, to slow down and appreciate the simple pleasures of a well-cooked meal.

Chef Mary knew that the success of her book relied on the support and enthusiasm of her readers. With a grateful heart, she dedicated "Authentic Italian Pasta Recipes" to all those who shared her love for Italian cuisine, encouraging them to embark on their own culinary adventures and create their own stories through the joy of cooking.

Chef Mary Doe's journey to preserve the legacy of Italian pasta was a testament to her deep-rooted passion and unwavering commitment. Through her book, she hoped to keep the flavors of Italy alive, one delicious recipe at a time.

With a final touch of love and gratitude, Chef Mary looked at her completed work, knowing that her labor of love would be a treasured companion for pasta lovers, home cooks, and anyone seeking to bring the taste of Italy into their own kitchen.

Thank you, dear readers, for joining Chef Mary Doe on this culinary journey through "Authentic Italian Pasta Recipes." May it inspire you to discover the magic of Italian cuisine and create unforgettable moments around the table. Buon appetito!